145
69

THE STEADFAST MAN

To

ADELA ROGERS ST JOHNS

THE
STEADFAST
MAN

a life of St Patrick

PAUL GALLICO

London
MICHAEL JOSEPH

First published by
MICHAEL JOSEPH LTD
26 Bloomsbury Street,
London, W.C.1
1958

© *copyright 1958 by Paul Gallico*

Set and printed in Great Britain by Tonbridge Printers Ltd, Peach
Hall Works, Tonbridge, Kent, in Bembo twelve on thirteen point,
on paper made by Henry Bruce at Currie, Midlothian, and bound
by James Burn at Esher, Surrey

ACKNOWLEDGEMENTS

Grateful acknowledgement is hereby made for generous help, encouragement and assistance rendered in the research and preparation for this book, by the Rev. John Brady, Dunboyne, Co. Meath; the Very Reverend Timothy Connolly, St Columban's, Dalgan Park, Navan, Co. Meath; Rev. Patrick J. Corish, Maynooth College, Co. Kildare; John M. Durr, Frenchpark, Co. Roscommon; Professor Delargy, Irish Folklore Commission, Dublin; Patrick Hughes, Browne & Nolan Co., Dublin; Dr G. Hayes McCoy, Curator, National Museum, Dublin; Rev. Francis MacLarnon, St Patrick's Academy, Dungannon, Co. Tyrone; Dr T. F. G. Paterson, Curator, Museum, Armagh; Arthur Pollock Esq., Cathedral House, Downpatrick; Dr Thomas Wall, Librarian, Irish Folklore Commission, Dublin.

PAUL GALLICO

Nihil obstat:
Andreas Moore, L.C.L.
Censor deputatus

Imprimatur:
E. Morragh Bernard, Vic. Gen.
Westmonasterii, die 11a Januarii, 1958

CONTENTS

Introduction

'ALTHOUGH I am imperfect in many things,' wrote Saint Patrick of Ireland, shortly before laying down cross and crozier for the last time, 'I nevertheless wish that my brethren and kinsmen should know what sort of person I am, so that they may understand my heart's desire.'

Annually on March 17th in New York, there is held a St Patrick's Day parade that proceeds up one of the city's main and most beautiful arteries, Fifth Avenue, past the tall, twin spires of St Patrick's Cathedral, a long line of marchers consisting of Irish Societies, many bands, some of the military, the police, city officials, prominent Irishmen, pipers, gaily clad children in Irish costume. Vendors do a land-office business with green pennants and flags with the golden harp of Ireland imprinted on them, green ribbons, green-dyed carnations, and artificial shamrocks.

Few, are aware that this green, 'The Wearing of the Green,' is a symbol not of the lush meadows and foliage of the Emerald Isle, but of an ancient Celtic fertility rite, the burning of green leaves, or green boughs, representing the spirit of vegetation, the ashes of which when carried forth and spread over the fields would make them fruitful.

More may have been taught, or believe, that the shamrock is worn because, during the days of his ministry in Ireland, Patrick used the three leaves to illustrate the nature of the Holy Trinity, a legend, like so many connected with Patrick,

9

borne out by no evidence and never so much as hinted at by Patrick himself in the two documents he left behind composed and written by himself.

Such myths and beliefs do no harm. But it is sad to reflect that probably not one in a thousand of the many parading, or lining the sidewalks, on the line of march of Irish name, parentage, or ancestry comprehend what sort of person their Saint was, or—as he wished them to know—what was his heart's desire.

March 17th, the day acknowledged by all sources as the one on which the Saint died in an indeterminate year towards the end of the fifth century A.D. inaugurates a three-day period of devotion in Ireland. Every Irish schoolchild is taught that St Patrick was born somewhere in Britain in the year A.D. 385; that when he was a boy of sixteen he was kidnapped by Irish raiders and carried off into slavery from whence he escaped after six years; and that he returned to Ireland in A.D. 432, converted the Irish and died in A.D. 461.

That this chronology is in grave dispute is unimportant against the fact that in Ireland itself there is misunderstanding as what manner of person was their patron Saint and what motivated the devotion of half of his life and perhaps more to the service of God through service to them.

Patrick is loved in Ireland; he is the most popular Saint. He has lent his name to hundreds upon hundreds of thousands of Irish children. Annual pilgrimages and retreats are conducted to and at shrines or localities connected with his presence there during his mission. He has left his mark upon the people and upon the land, and is one of those 'living' Saints whose vibrations still echo after fifteen centuries.

But as to how he lives, and in what manner of person, in some parts of Ireland, would surely horrify Patrick were he to sit in a cottage in Connemara, Ulster, or Meath and listen to an old man tell tales of a figure who emerges as a vengeful and irascible old magician stumping the country bestowing curses in equal measure with blessings, blasting and slaying and, in one monstrous tale, murdering his own sister by ordering his chariot driven over her thrice in punishment for her sins.

In this instance it is not ignorance that has given rise to a wholly false picture of this gentle and self-effacing apostle but rather the mythopoeic instinct of a people who some-times wove outrageous legends about their own heroes in pre-Christian times, and who, though converted by Patrick to belief in Christ, were, as many other peoples, never wholly parted from the memories of their earlier religion. The Irish came to Christianity with a long baggage-train of myths, rites, superstitions and heritage. They embraced Christianity with enthusiasm. Nevertheless, a good deal of the old luggage continued to lie about the house.

St Patrick converted a nation whose culture and history lay embedded in the grey matter contained in the skulls of a class of educated men, Druids, poets, teachers, lawyers, etc. Poetry was a living thing—song and story around the camp fire, or in the banqueting hall. Tradition and knowledge were passed on by word of mouth from teacher to pupil, from father to son.

Along with the Gospel, Patrick brought book culture to Ireland, the Latin alphabet, the Latin language. Scholarship, which heretofore had relied upon memory, took to the written word and in some aspects outshone that of the Continent from whence it had come. Irish monastic scholar-ship has left its mark upon Europe. At the same time, the Irish, and in particular the less educated, never relinquished their ancient habit of the handed-down tale. Irish folk-lore itself is a lifelong study of enchanting interest.

In the telling of these tales, and in the writings of monastic hacks attempting to produce 'edifying' and moral stories— early Christian times were apparently as exposed to literary trash as our own days—the character of St Patrick became distorted beyond all recognition. There were probably legends already in circulation about him during his lifetime —exaggerations as there are about every great man as he accumulates years. With the centuries these have become amplified, encrusted and solidified . . . and as false as the physical representation of him in statuary and illustration. He was so much greater, more wonderful, more admirable.

Even in his lifetime, St Patrick, as well as Patrick the man and missionary, was misunderstood, misrepresented and slandered so that he was forced to defend himself against his detractors in Britain, in France and in Ireland itself.

To all this has been added recently the clamour of disputing scholars, philologists, antiquarians, historians, learned and expert in their field, but who, like the myth-makers and tale-tellers, in pursuit of their ends and their profession have lost the man, and also the Saint; for all Saints were first men, with all of the strengths and the weaknesses, the turpitude and nobility, to be found intermingled in the human being.

This book is an attempt to present St Patrick somewhat as he was—or might have been from his own testimony and the little, backed by evidence, that is truly known about him.

It is not usual to suggest that a book be read backwards, but appended to this volume are translations by Prof. Ludwig Bieler of the two great, authentic Patrician documents written by the hand of St Patrick himself and which have survived in copies, of which one is to be found in the Book of Armagh, preserved in the Library of Trinity College in Dublin.

One is the *Confessio*, or Confession of St Patrick, as he himself referred to it, and the other his *Letter To The Soldiers of Coroticus*.

'This is my confession before I die,' is how Patrick ends the first work, but it is more than a mere 'confession'; it is a testament of his labours, a self-defence, and a thanksgiving to God conceived on a simultaneously grand and humble scale. Here and there it is interlarded with fascinating biographical flashes and glimpses. It is studded with quotations from Scripture. The style is that of a man of action unfamiliar with the subtleties of the pen and the regimen and formats necessary to writers. It is often rambling and inconsequent, though here copyists may sometimes be at fault. Certain passages are obscure. They were written by an old man, a hurt and sensitive old man looking back over a long, adventurous and dedicated life.

The second, the Letter, is a flamingly angry epistle of denunciation and excommunication written to the soldiers of a Welsh chieftain, Coroticus, but against Coroticus himself and meant to be read in his presence, or in the presence of his friends and supporters. It was prompted by the fact that the soldiers of Coroticus—nominally Christians, though there is indication that their ranks consisted of a rag-tag of apostates, heathen, hard men and adventurers for booty, who reversed the more familiar proceeding by raiding the Irish coast from the British—had come upon a flock of Patrick's newly baptised Christians, slaughtered a number and sold the rest into slavery to heathen nations. One of these nations was the Franks who at that time had not yet been led by Clovis into the Church.

Embedded in these two documents is to be found the true personality of a man who, like other great bearers of the message of the Gospels, was not to be stilled by the crushing weight of the centuries and to whose achievements the Irish nation and people of today are a living monument.

A quick preliminary perusal of these might supply the first hint as to the nature of this truly great and devoted missionary, and enable you to be at one with the author in his attempt to re-create something of the true St Patrick out of the debris of time and the ashes of conquest; and, from the meagre sources that might be considered trustworthy, to present him as he appears in truth to have been.

A re-reading of them, when you have done with this book, might then well confirm a different picture of one of the greatest of Christian apostles.

> Paul Gallico,
> Ashford Castle,
> Cong,
> County Mayo,
> Eire.

CHAPTER ONE

The Young Patrick

I

'There was in the country of Airthir a certain rich and honourable man named Daire. To him Patrick made request that he would grant him some place for the exercise of religion. And the rich man said to the Saint, "What place dost thou desire?" "I desire," said the Saint, "that thou grant me that high ground which is called the Ridge of the Willow, and I shall build there a place." But he was unwilling to give the Saint that high ground; but he gave him another place, on lower ground, where is now The Church of the Relics near Ardd-Machae: and there Saint Patrick dwelt with his people. . . .

'And after these things Daire came to pay his respects to Saint Patrick, bringing with him a wonderful bronze pot holding three gallons that had come from beyond the seas. And Daire said to the Saint, "Lo, this bronze pot is for thee." And St Patrick said "Grazacham!" [So sounded the colloquial expression of the Latin Gratias Agamus: Let us give thanks.] And when Daire returned to his own house, he said, "That stupid man, who said nothing more civil than Grazacham in return for a wonderful bronze three-gallon pot." And Daire then proceeded to say to his servants, "Go and bring us back our pot." So they went and said to Patrick, "We are going to take away the pot." Nevertheless, St Patrick, that time too said, "Grazacham, Take it away." And they took it away. And Daire questioned his companions and said, "What did the Christian say when ye took back the pot?" And they answered, "He just said Grazacham." Daire answered and said, "Grazacham when it is given! Grazacham when it is taken away! His expression is so good that his pot must be brought back to him with his Grazacham." And Daire came himself this time and

15

brought the pot to Patrick saying, "Thy pot must remain with thee; for
thou art a steadfast and unchangeable man; moreover, as for that parcel
of ground which thou didst once desire, I give it to thee now, in so far
as I possess it, and do thou dwell there."'

LIFE OF ST PATRICK, by Muirchu, A.D. 699

'*Constant in the fear of God and steadfast in his faith*
'*On him the Church is built as on Peter;*
'*And his apostleship has he received from God—*
'*The gates of Hell will not prevail against him.*'

HYMN ON ST PATRICK, TEACHER OF THE IRISH,
St Secundinus (Contemporary)

MAGONUS SUCATUS PATRICIUS, later to be known as St
Patrick, apostle of Ireland, the man of steadfast faith, of
steadfast and unchanging determination, was born somewhere in Roman Britain, some time early in the fifth
century, or late in the fourth. He was a Christian, born into
a country but recently Christianised, a part of the dying
Roman Empire in which the State religion was now
Christianity.

Patrick and his family considered themselves not Britons,
but Romans. Their civil allegiance was to the Roman
emperor, and the seat of government, Rome. Their spiritual
obedience was to the highest ecclesiastical authority, the
Bishop of Rome, the Pope. Their ways, laws, customs were
Roman and they were defended by the Roman Army.
Though they spoke the native Brythonic tongue, Latin was
the language of universal intercourse, both civil and ecclesi-
astic, and no man could hope to succeed in Romano-Britain,
in commerce, politics or religion, without a thorough
groundwork and knowledge of both written and spoken
Latin. It was this lack of good Latin foundation that was to
haunt Patrick throughout his life.

Patrick was a free-born Roman citizen of a well-to-do landed family boasting patents of minor nobility. His father was a Decurion, a local official of the national government and a deacon of the Christian Church. His name was Calpornius. Patrick's grandfather, still living when Patrick was a boy, was named Potitus and was an ordained priest.

So much Patrick tells us himself in the opening paragraph of his *Confessio* written in his old age in Ireland: 'I am Patrick, a sinner, most unlearned, the least of all the faithful and utterly despised by many. My father was Calpornius, a deacon, son of Potitus, a priest, of the village Bannavem Taburniae; he had a small farm hard by, where I was taken captive.' In the early days of Christianity in Britain, celibacy was not imposed upon the clergy.

All that is actually known about Patrick, his family, his early life and education, and what manner of man he was, is contained in surviving copies of two documents known to have been composed by him, the *Confessio*, a *Letter to the Soldiers of Coroticus*, a few fragments, some Canons, and an adulatory hymn written about him by one of his disciples during his lifetime. Every other document, source or 'Life' of the Saint was compiled or written at the earliest some 200 years after Patrick's death, many from sources in themselves not entirely reliable. Most of them were no more than pious fiction or collections of miracles supposed to have been performed by Patrick from his earliest days when he was yet an infant.

The young Patrick by his own admission was far from a saint. His references to himself throughout his Confession as a sinner are in the mood and style of apostolic and religious writing of his day and times, but he admits that he turned from God as a youth, that he did not keep His commandments or obey the priests, and that not only

Christian but secular teaching went in one ear and out of the other. He must have been a scandal to his grandfather, old Potitus the Priest, who no doubt lectured him and prophesied a bad end for him unless he mended his ways. The younger generation in Bannavem Taburniae, it seems, was exactly what it is in every age and in every land.

The boy sinned too, not only in the literary sense, but physically, for in his rambling and otherwise disjointed memoir he refers to a wrong done in his boyhood—'one day, nay, in one hour because I was not yet strong. I know not—God knoweth—whether I was then fifteen years old; and I did not believe in the living God, nor did I so from childhood, but lived in death and unbelief until I was severely chastised and severely humiliated, by hunger and nakedness, and that daily.' The memory of this sin—and what it was is never revealed—remained with him to the end of his days. Thirty years after its commission, it returned to haunt him, influence the direction of his life and demand its price.

The mists of time have descended upon the place of Patrick's birth and cannot be lifted. It has been argued from the Rock of Dumbarton in Scotland to the headlands of Wales, the beaches of Boulogne and the plains of Central Spain, and positive identification of the spot where the infant first opened his eyes and uttered his first cries still eludes every biographer as it has in the past, whether he be scholar, cleric or poet.

The desire to visit the birthplace of a great human who has appealed to our senses or our hearts, is an attempt to reach to the core of the person, to understand him and make him ours. Genius and sublimity remain an eternal mystery. Could we but stand where the departed one was born to look upon the four walls that first enclosed him, see the conformation of the land, the shape of the hills or the plain,

the streams, torrents or rivers that divided it, hear the songs
of the birds and the sounds made by wind or water, raging
winter storms or the peaceful rustle of trees or palm fronds,
could we but breathe the air of that place, then some of the
mystery might be penetrated and the secret revealed to us.

At least, noting the sights that he saw, treading the
ground, inhaling the fragrances, or sharing the misery and
squalor, if such there was, we can draw closer to him, understand his memories, nostalgias and longings and glean
something of the natural background that helped to form
his character.

With regard to the birthplace of Patrick, the centuries
have obliterated every clue. It is thought most likely to have
been in the valley of the Severn or even farther west in the
vicinity of the Bristol Channel. Gloucester was the northernmost limit of peaceful, organised Roman civilisation in
Britain, such civilisation as would have seen Patrick's father
as both a town and religious official of the community with
a farm or country seat near by.

But one thing is certain: that other dwelling, were it villa,
loggia, clay-walled farm or rich estate—lay close to the
Western ocean and was staffed with slaves and servants both
male and female. For it was while he was on a visit there
that Patrick and all the family retainers were swept up in the
net of the Irish raiders who came in from the sea, and carried
off to captivity and slavery.

Wherever it was, Patrick loved it; the memory of the spot
filled him with longing and homesickness during his days of
exile. He had a second home, too, to which he was drawn
by strong ties and endearing memories. This was France—
Gaul—Auxerre, the very heart of that rich, fruitful land
where he studied for the priesthood. In his old age, thinking
upon his flock and what he had sacrificed for them, one

painful, nostalgic sigh bursts from him, who had always considered himself blessed by God to be allowed to be His fisherman in Pagan seas: 'Wherefore, then, even if I wished to leave them and go to Britain, how I would have loved to go to my country and my parents, and also to Gaul in order to visit the brethren and to see the face of the saints of my Lord! God knows it that I much desired it!'

Patrick spent half of his life in Ireland, but it was never home to him, its pagan inhabitants never anything to him but barbarians, his ministry there aught but exile from the scenes and the people he loved. His manuscript glows with love of God and Christ. It was this love that he succeeded in conveying to the Irish and which has never been extinguished in their breasts. But Patrick himself always remained a Roman and a missionary to the heathen.

Seen through the eye of retrospect as the devoted old apostle looks back upon his early youth, the young Patrick was wayward and a sinner. By other standards, he was a normal, healthy boy, spoiled perhaps by indulgent parents and a position of moderate wealth and social standing. He was not the first lad to neglect his schooling for the more fascinating attractions of nature and play, to turn a deaf ear to the strictures of heavy-handed elders, or to snooze through a long-winded sermon. Then he regarded it all gaily and with a light heart. It was only later that he took his transgressions more seriously.

He was of native Celtic stock, but like all boys of his era was given a Roman name and of course a Roman education. It is not known how much of it stuck or how much elementary Latin he absorbed; according to Patrick, very little. Yet, when a slave in Ireland, he soon enough learned to speak Gaelic and became familiar with all of the idioms of the local tongue.

Patrick was a fifth-century boy. He lived in a pleasant and adequate civilisation well supplied with creature comforts such as central heating, glass windows, hot and cold running baths, warm woollen cloth, tools and utensils, a more cultured table from the culinary point of view than Britain has been able to produce since, transportation on land by horse and chariot, on sea by sturdy enough sailing ships.

But, like Patrick's birthplace, the exact dates of his *floruit*, that is his life span, seem no longer identifiable. There is one school that argues cogently the birth of Patrick about the year 385, his coming to Ireland as a Bishop and a missionary in 432, and his death on March 17th, 461, at the age of seventy-six. There is a second group presenting equally convincing arguments that Patrick's obit was not 461, but 492, that he came to Ireland only in the year 461 and thereafter flourished for a little over thirty years as apostle to the heathen Irish before going to his reward. This would move his birth forward to around the year 416. Somewhere, due to the complications of Irish annals and careless interpreters and copyists, thirty years have been lost. The problem may never be resolved.

But if there remains doubt as to the dates of the birth and death of the St Patrick of the *Confessio*, the man who performed the monumental and near-miraculous work of transforming almost the whole of the Irish nation from Pagans to Christians, there is none as to his era, the conditions that prevailed in Britain in the fifth century and the state of Christianity.

'Roman rule,' wrote the venerable Bede, 'came to an end in Britain almost 470 years after the landing of Gaius Julius Caesar. [A.D. 409]' Rome had fallen to the Goths. The barbarian hordes were sweeping over the Continent. Western

Europe lay in chaos. The Roman Empire was all but destroyed. The one surviving comfort to man in this holocaust was the Christian religion and the Catholic Church.

If it were true that Patrick was born *circa* 385, then he lived in a Britain still defended against the Norse and Saxon raiders, the Picts (the Caledonians of the North) and the Scots (the Irish of the West) by the Roman Legions.

As a boy he would have looked with awe as the armoured legionaries, hard, brawny men from far-off lands, raised the dust about their standards with the tramp of marching feet. His ears would have been filled with braying of the *bucinae*, the rhythmic songs of the soldiers as they slogged along the road, and the rattle and clank of their armour. He would have looked with wonder at the great horsehair-crested helms, the regimental colours of the tunics and capes of men and officers, blues and scarlets and the majesty of the bronze eagles.

He might with his companions, in the year 400, have followed one such Century from its barracks, shouting and cheering as they marched away followed by their rumbling baggage tumbrels, unsuspecting that he would never see them again, that they were never to return and that now the once peaceful country of his youth lay defenceless before the three nations of raiders and invaders from north, east and west.

The disasters taking place on the Continent were far distant; communication was slow. They seemed just like others in a series of invasions, repulsions, conquests, revolts and battles that had been going on for years. The shattering of an empire can only be seen in retrospect. Yet the parents of Patrick must have looked with unease upon the departure of the Legions to fight the Goths and the Huns in France and Italy. Decurio Calpornius may have been one of a local committee to sign his name to a petition to the Emperor Honorius to send the Legions back, since, under the dictatorship of the Empire, Britons had not been permitted to bear or train in arms.

Honorius sent back word that henceforth the Britons must take care of themselves as best they could and organise their own defences.

If Patrick was born and lived at the later date, he grew up in a southern England already denuded of defence and without a trained soldiery, yet a Britain that still considered itself a Roman province and its people Roman citizens. They remained Christians in religion and Romans in thought and civil life; but the clash of sword and spear on shield and the war cries of their enemies sounded ever closer.

Yet one knows that life went on and that many Britons could not believe the Romans had deserted them. On the Continent, even though in its death throes, the Empire was still behaving like the Empire, and both Bede and Probus report that in the year 432 the Roman Pontiff Celestine sent Bishop Palladius to the Scots (Irish) who believed in Christ, to be their first Bishop. Patrick then could have been sixteen.

In the year 446, in the reign of Theodosius the Younger, the unhappy Britons sent a letter to Aetius, a third-time Roman Consul: 'To Aetius, thrice Consul, come the groans of the Britons. The barbarians drive us into the sea and the sea drives us back to the barbarians. Between these, two deadly alternatives confront us, drowning or slaughter.'

There was yet a third alternative, equally fearful—kidnapping and slavery. And this was what befell Patrick in the sixteenth year of his life, whether in 401, or 432, makes little difference to his story or his life. The forts that once guarded the mouth of the Severn and the coast of the Bristol

Channel, the barracks that once housed the invincible Legions, stood equally empty. Britain lay open to raiders from every quarter.

However, there is a neat bit of irony offered by the later date of Patrick's *Floruit*. It would mean that in the same year that the Pope sent Palladius, the first Bishop to reach Ireland from France to attend the needs of the few scattered Christian communities and families living in the south-eastern part of Ireland—an episcopacy said not to have been a success, and lasting only a few years when Palladius is reported to have been killed, or died—the real and eventual Apostle of Ireland was bound thither, likewise wild-eyed, scratched, beaten, bleeding, bound hand and foot in the bottom of the vessel of Irish pirates and sea raiders, captive along with more than a thousand of his countrymen.

II

'. . . *he had a country seat nearby, and there I was taken captive.*

'*I was then about sixteen years of age. I did not know the true God. I was taken into captivity to Ireland with many thousands of people—and deservedly so.*'

'*As a youth, nay, almost as a boy, not able to speak, I was taken captive, before I knew what to pursue and what to avoid.*'

'*On the other hand, I did not go to Ireland of my own accord, not until I had nearly perished; but this was rather for my good for thus I was purged by the Lord; and He made me fit so that I might now be what was once far from me.*'

St Patrick: 'CONFESSIO'

THE last paragraph above, from Patrick's own narrative has been variously interpreted, but it may with reason be assumed that it refers to the fact that he fought like a young wildcat when surprised on the beach or at the seaside villa of

his parents and had to be subdued and trussed before he
could be tossed into the bottom of one of the raider's ships
with the rest of the captives. That he was not killed was
becouse he was young and strong and of the commercial
value of several cows, the medium of exchange in Ireland.
The Irish raids upon the British coast were sparked not by
animosity but by business.

Thousands of captives were taken at the same time as himself, Patrick reports; there must have been at least a hundred
ships in the flotilla.

It was in summer-time they came, when the body of
water that the British West-coast dwellers called the 'Western
Sea' could be as smooth and friendly as an inland lough,
compared to the fierce anger of its winter aspect, when no
ships ventured from the harbours to risk a passage.

They could have come stealthily by night by moon or
starlight, with no man to know or give warning until, as
they swept in from the sea and rounded some dark, sheltering
headland, the fearful braying of their bronze, calabash-shaped
war-trumpets—you may see these same trumpets in the
National Museum in Dublin—awoke the unsuspecting and
unarmed inhabitants to terror, slaughter and captivity.

They beached their ships miles apart as the two anchors
of a net and, working by the light of the farms they had set
aflame, herded their human prey into the trap. The old were
butchered, the too-young ignored, those who resisted were
battered into insensibility; everything movable was carried
from the houses down to the ships as loot, along with the
human spoils.

By sunrise, the brown-sailed fleet of red and hairy men
glutted with blood and booty would be standing out to sea,
safe from pursuit, with their cargo of the living, leaving
behind them on the mainland the dead lying in the ashes of

their homes. They were rough, brutal warriors, these island pirates, pagans without pity, tenderness or mercy. What exquisite irony, indeed, that on this raid they carried with them the instrument of their own taming, a beardless, beaten boy who, single-handed and with no weapon other than a crooked staff, steadfast purpose and invincible faith, was to subdue them and all their kind and alter the spiritual nature of their island home for ever.

Story, legend and conjecture have several of St Patrick's sisters also taken captive in the same raid and conveyed to Ireland, and the suggestion has been made that his parents were killed by the pirates. . . . There is no evidence to support any of these tales.

On the contrary, Patrick himself makes no mention of any sisters, brothers or near relatives taken with him in his own brief accounts of the event given in *Confessio* and the *Letter*. Indeed, in the latter, he indicates that when he returned voluntarily to Ireland as a missionary, his parents were still living—'. . . out of love for my neighbours and sons [the Irish] for whom I gave up my country and parents and my life to the point of death.'

And later in another portion of the scorchingly indignant *Letter*, he writes: 'Did I come to Ireland without God or according to the flesh? I am bound by the Spirit not to see any of my kinsfolk. Is it of my own doing that I have holy mercy on the people who once took me captive and made away with the servants and maids of my father's house.'

Into 'maids,' one could, if one wished, read 'young girls' or 'virgins,' who could have been his sisters, but it would seem that Patrick, having mentioned his father's house and thus referred to him directly, would equally have referred to his sister or sisters had they been kidnapped at the same time as he. It may be assumed that Patrick alone was taken in this fatal raid and alone was being borne to dwell in a strange country amidst a strange people.

There are two natural small boat harbours in Ireland for which a shallow-draught raiding fleet would make for safe anchorage and the easy disembarking of goods and humans. One is Strangford Lough in County Down, entered by a narrow neck just east of what is today Downpatrick, and the other Larne Lough, north of Belfast, where access is equally narrow and the anchorage protected.

Patrick himself provides no clue as to what was the first Irish landfall to sadden his eyes, whether the peaks of the Wicklow Range looming up behind the seaboard plain, or the empurpled, melancholy Mountains of Mourne to the north. Behind the coastal flats of eastern Ireland with their bays, loughs and estuaries rise forbidding mountain barriers, mysterious and threatening when seen from the approaches of the sea.

He is equally reticent as to the name of the Chieftain, Lord, Druid or master to whom he was sold as a slave and the whereabouts of his captivity. Indeed, the only place-names mentioned in either document are Bannavem Taburniae where his family lived, and the Woods of Focluth whence came his call to return and baptise the Irish; and the accuracy of both of these is open to doubt.

Tradition, other sources and the indications of common sense suggest most strongly that Patrick's owner was a Pictish Chieftain of northern Dalaradia by the name of Miliucc, said also to have been a Druid, the place of his captivity Mounts Skerry and Slemish, and the harbour of his landing Larne, north of what is today Belfast. Larne is only a few miles from the area about Mount Slemish and it would have been no difficulty for Miliucc to have journeyed to that seaport to purchase some household slaves and labourers, amongst whom was Patrick, who by his own testimony became a shepherd.

This bondage lasted six years. During this period Patrick found God and God found Patrick and thereafter, to the end of the Saint's days, neither ever abandoned the other. No man ever served God more faithfully, intensely and unswervingly than Patrick. God preserved the life of Patrick against many dangers and used him as His instrument to bring a great and noble people to Christianity.

In loneliness, in despair, in hunger and in cold, and above all in the abject misery of slavery, with the loss of all personal sense of existence, dignity and pride, the boy Patrick turned to Him who, he had been told, had proved Himself the friend and solace of the poor, the humbled and the thralled. Like many men before him and after, Patrick found himself closer to God on a mountain top.

He tried to remember all of the Christian religion he had been taught at home and to which he had paid so little attention. He prayed; he fasted; he gave himself up whole-heartedly, body and soul, to God with no doubts or reservations.

Of this period he writes himself: 'But after I came to Ireland, every day I had to tend sheep, and many times a day I prayed . . . the love of God and His fear came to me more and more, and my faith was strengthened. And my spirit was moved so that in a single day I would say as many as a hundred prayers, and almost as many in the night, and this even when I was staying in the woods and on the mountain; and I used to get up for prayer before daylight, through snow, through frost, through rain, and I felt no harm, and there was no sloth in me, as I now see because the spirit within me was then fervent.'

In return for this fervency, God gave him comfort, endurance, courage and, in the end, freedom.

III

THE lives of the remarkable men whom we choose to recognise or canonise as Saints are filled with mysteries, sometimes in the shape of the suspension of natural laws, called miracles, others in the form of direct communication with God which is denied to lesser souls. In none of his writings did Patrick ever lay claim to working a miracle, but there was no doubt in his mind that he received messages from the Creator and that these messages showed him to be selected for an especial purpose.

The first such communication he received while with his flock on the slopes of Slemish. 'And there one night I heard in my sleep a voice saying to me: "It is well that you fast, soon you will go to your own country." And again, after a short while, I heard a voice saying to me: "See, your ship is ready." And it was not near, but at a distance of perhaps two hundred miles, and I had never been there, nor did I know a living soul there; and then I took flight, and I left the man with whom I had stayed six years. And I went in the strength of God who directed my way to my good and I feared nothing until I came to that ship.'

The homesick boy, an escaped slave and a marked man, foot-slogged his way through forest and bog southwards and to the sea coast until he came to a seaport which would have been near where Wicklow is now by the mouth of the River Vartry.

The journey itself was in the nature of a miracle. He was ever in danger of recapture, of attack by men whose lands he crossed, or by wild beasts, hunger, thirst and fatigue.

Armoured by his conviction that God had sent him and was watching over him, nothing could touch him and nothing did.

At the seaport the mystery was continued. A ship was afloat and ready to sail. In those days, the light vessels, often flat-bottomed, were beached on the tidal flats for loading. You may see such flats by Baldoyle and Portmarnock outside Dublin where the sea recedes for miles. When the tide came in, the skin-covered curraghs were refloated, the brown linen sails hoisted and they skimmed off over the water, faster and often more seaworthy in a blow than heavier-timbered craft.

The barque that God had selected for Patrick's transportation from Ireland was a trading ship. Its cargo consisted of the great, long-limbed, shaggy, savage Irish wolf-hounds highly valued on the Continent, and particularly in France, as hunting dogs. Patrick would have been quite familiar with these animals and fearless in his approach to and handling of them, but the huge, snapping, snarling beasts collected amidships of the craft must have been a terror to the sailors manning the ship. Patrick offered to work his passage.

'And the day that I arrived the ship was set afloat, and I said that I was able to pay for my passage with them. But the captain was not pleased, and with indignation he answered harshly: "It is of no use for you to ask to go along with us." And when I heard this I left them in order to return to the hut where I was staying. And as I went I began to pray, and before I had ended my prayer, I heard one of them shouting behind me, "Come, hurry, we shall take you on in good faith; make friends with us in whatever way you like." And so on that day I refused to suck their breasts for fear of God [an ancient Irish and Pagan rite of submission and seeking protection], but rather hoped they would come to the faith of Jesus Christ, because they were pagans. And thus I had my way with them and we set sail at once.'

What of the 'hut' to which Patrick refers and where he was staying. Was it occupied by Christians? And was this one of the secrets of the escape from the north and the privations of hunger? There were already Christian colonies on the east coast of Ireland. Was there a kind of underground railway that handed Patrick on from Christian family to Christian family, providing him with food, shelter and directions? Patrick does not say. But one of the characteristics of the *Confessio* is the great number of things which we would dearly love to know about the Saint and which he, writing in his old age and gazing with uncertain memory down the long, confusing corridors of more than seventy years, does not tell. The work is full of incoherencies—events remembered and set down out of sequence and context—and takes for granted things, places and events known to his contemporary readers, but which fifteen centuries have all but obliterated for us.

But in this instance the scene on the salt tidal flats by the mouth of the Vartry against the background peak of Mt Brockagh is crystal-clear. The berry-brown, leather-toughened, un-Irish-looking boy, finding the ship already afloat and the sailors at their work of preparing to cast off with a wary eye upon the savage, uneasy cargo, applies for passage and a job. And perhaps, to show his fitness for the work and his familiarity with the beasts, he jumps down amidst the beasts, slapping their jaws and flanks in friendly fashion, roughing their great heads and ears. The uneasy hounds, recognising a friend in their midst, become quiet and tractable.

The captain is less so. The youth has much against him in the Ireland of that day and era. He is a stranger; he is a

Christian known to be staying with Christians. He may be an escaped slave. In the eyes of the captain he spells trouble. All this would have developed the moment that Patrick refused to suck their breasts.

Yet the moment that Patrick turns away, undismayed, praying, the dogs begin to mill and whine, snapping and snarling. The captain capitulates and sends a sailor running after Patrick to call him back on his own terms. Sail is hoisted and Patrick standing in the stern sees the country that has been cruel and harsh to him, abused and oppressed him and robbed him of six years of his youth, fading into the blue haze of the mountains, diminishing and at last vanishing altogether from sight. He has no kindly thoughts towards this land and its people at this moment. He does not believe that he has left anything of himself behind. This is escape. But it was only the beginning of a journey into a more stern and taxing bondage that was to last to the end of his days.

There were calm, smooth seas and fair winds and in three days the Irish traders touched the shores of France to find the country a desert, the scorched earth of war. Patrick does not give the place of the landing, but continues in his narrative mood of the moment: 'After three days we reached land, and for twenty-eight days we travelled through deserted country. And they lacked food and hunger overcame them; and the next day the captain said to me: "Tell me, Christian: you say that your God is great and all-powerful; why, then, do you not pray for us. As you can see we are suffering from hunger; it is unlikely indeed that we shall ever see a human being again."

'I said to them full of confidence: "Be truly converted with all your heart to the Lord my God, because nothing is impossible for Him, that this day He may send you food on your way until you be satisfied; for He has abundance

everywhere." And with the help of God, so it came to pass:
suddenly a herd of pigs appeared on the road before our
eyes, and they killed many of them; and there they stopped
for two nights and fully recovered their strength, and their
hounds received their fill, for many of them had grown weak
and were half-dead along the way. And from that day they
had plenty of food. They also found some wild honey, and
offered some of it to me, and one of them said: "This we
offer in sacrifice." Thanks be to God, I tasted none of it.'

A boy of twenty-two, starved, and with a sweet tooth,
refusing honey since it had been offered as a Pagan sacrifice!
Already the steadfast man appears.

'That same night,' Patrick continues this one consecutive
narrative sequence in the entire *Confessio*, 'when I was asleep,
Satan assailed me violently, a thing I shall remember as long
as I shall be in this body. And he fell upon me like a huge
rock, and I could not stir a limb.' Satan it may have been,
but the symptoms more amusingly resemble those of a
severe nightmare resulting from indigestion due, after a
period of starvation, to over-eating of fresh-killed pork.

Yet to Patrick it became translated into a religious experience. For he called upon Helias—or Elias or Eli—the copyists
here having possibly made free with Patrick's original word-
ing of the Being on which he called in his terror at the
seizure. As one in the grip of a nightmare he was shouting
in his sleep when the sun came up and its warmth and splendour freed him of all misery, and he believed that he had
been sustained by Christ.

The company then continued on its way, now under the
protection of Patrick's God, for He gave them food and fire
along the road and dry weather every day until just at the
end of the tenth day, as their food ran out again, they came
once more to an inhabited portion of the country and

B

encountered people and their troubles and tribulations were over.

Where had they landed? Where had this journey taken place? No one will ever know. If the early chronology ascribed to Patrick's life be correct, his arrival in France coincides with the sweep through that unhappy country by the Vandals who moved like a brush-fire through the land leaving nothing growing or standing behind them. If it occurred thirty years later, the land might still not have recovered from repeated devastation as Gaul and all Europe entered the chaos of the dark age of barbarism and classic Gaul vanished for ever.

It is believed that a three days' sail, seventy-two hours at an average of ten miles an hour, would have brought the traders to the south coast of France in the vicinity of the tidal marshes and flats of Bordeaux not dissimilar to the Irish strand familiar to the sailors. And a month's journey across France would have carried them to Italy. And there Patrick vanishes completely for 'a few years.'

IV

YET one faint light beams to us through the darkness of Patrick's whereabouts between the time he took leave of the Irish captain and his comrades, and his own report of his return to Britain. In the prefix of the work of the Irish monk, Tirechàn, eighth-century compiler of a memoir on some of the travels and work of St Patrick and his church foundations in Ireland, and also appearing in the great Book of Armagh, are three disconnected 'Sayings of St Patrick' which the chronicler had either from some now lost written source, or from his master, Bishop Ultan, who commissioned Tirechàn's work.

One of them places the twenty-two-year-old escaped slave in France, Italy, and that area now known as the Côte d'Azur—the saying: 'The fear of God I had as my guide through Gaul and Italy and the islands in the Tyrrhene Sea' [the Mediterranean].

It is this saying or fragment that is the basis, along with a further report of Tirechàn's on Bishop Ultan's authority, for placing Patrick on the Monastery Island of Lerins founded by Honoratus, a monk and scholar.

There appears to be no document or evidence of record that Patrick ever studied or was present at the Monastery of Lerins beyond Tirechàn's report of something Bishop Ultan knew or had read more than two hundred years following the death of Patrick, who himself never referred to this island refuge.

Yet there is an odd link that has persisted down through the centuries, one that seems to be bound up in the apocryphal legend that St Patrick drove the snakes out of Ireland. He did not, but Honoratus DID drive the snakes out of Lerinus.

Bede, writing at the beginning of the eighth century, is probably the first to refer in literature to the non-existence of snakes in Ireland. It is also a fascinating mystery that Bede, the first of the great historians of Church and Christianity, fails to make any mention whatsoever of St Patrick or his mission and work amongst the Irish, though he does echo Probus in stating that the Roman Pontiff Celestine sent Palladius to the Scots (Irish) who believed in Christ to be their first Bishop.

Referring to Ireland and its reptiles, Bede writes: 'Ireland is broader than Britain and its mild, healthy climate is superior. Snow rarely lies longer than three days, so that there is no need to store hay in summer for winter use, or to build stables for beasts. There are no reptiles and no snake can exist there; for although often brought over from Britain, as soon as the ship nears land, they breathe its scented air and die. In fact almost everything in this isle enjoys immunity to poison, and I have heard that folk suffering from snake-bite have drunk water in which scrapings from the leaves of books from Ireland have been steeped, and that this remedy checked the spreading poison and reduced the swelling. The island abounds in milk and honey, and there is no lack of vines, fish and birds, while deer and goats are widely hunted.'

If Bede's *Pharmacopiae* and *Natural History* reflect the age during which he wrote and flourished, the fact that Ireland for whatever reason did not support snakes was known to him and writers long before him such as Orosius and Tacitus.

At the same time, it seems to have been known before and ever since the time of Honoratus, a Gallic prelate who had spent much time in the East, that the little island of Lerinus, lying beyond that of Lero, off the cape of Cannes, in the Provence area of the South of France, was uninhabit-able because it was a mass of tangled undergrowth infested with snakes.

Honoratus, or St Honoratus, as he became, selected this island to build a monastic retreat, cleaned out the under-brush, cleared the island of snakes, lizards and scorpions, dug wells, planted vines, built cells and refectory and founded there a monastery which became famous for the saints, bishops and scholars who spent time there. It became distinguished in the region almost immediately.

The date of its foundation cannot be ascertained, the first years of the fifth century being suggested. Since we are aware of the two chronologies for Patrick, one of which places his birth *circa* A.D. 385 and the other thirty years later, it is fruitless to speculate that Patrick might even have been a labourer during the clearing of the island and the foundation of the famous monastery.

But the mere fact of there being no snakes in Ireland and the possible historical placing of Patrick upon *another* island from which snakes *were* driven in the course of its clearing could be sufficient for legend shaping about his figure to confuse the two islands and even the two men and transfer the episode of the banishing of the snakes from Honoratus to Patrick and from Lerinus to Ireland.

Speculation upon various periods in the life of St Patrick may be endless, and often fruitless, when it comes to shedding light upon the personality and character of the man. Yet there remains a fascination about that isolated sentence, remembered or somewhere written down that has survived the centuries: 'The fear of God I had as my guide through Gaul and Italy and the islands in the Tyrrhene sea,' since it refers obviously to his first journey in France, the one undertaken with the Irish traders who facilitated his escape.

For this journey, instead of returning him to the home in Britain for which he had so longed and towards which his escape was directed, took him ever farther away from it, as far east as Italy and the *islands*—there were also monastic cells and establishments upon Lero, the sister island of Lerinus —in the Tyrrhenian Sea.

The fear of God was the boy's guide during the wanderings of several years, friendless and penniless amongst strangers who spoke a strange language and where the only universal speech was the Latin of the scholars, of which Patrick had no more than a smattering. But there was more than merely the fear of God to be his guide; there was the recent discovery of and yielding himself up to God.

For it must be remembered that the great dramatic and

physical adventure of the escape from Ireland and bondage to find himself once more a free man coincided with the greatest emotional experience in his life and a new kind of slavery, that of and to the word and spirit of Christ.

In a short space of time—perhaps the first recognition of conversion on the wintry slopes of Slemish was a matter of minutes—a young boy had shed the skin of his old character and adopted another. He had become aware not only of the slothful and sinful nature of his old life and personality, and of the punishment he was now suffering therefor, but also of where help and salvation lay. Furthermore, the seal had been set upon this remarkable experience by a manifestation to him of the mercy and forgiveness of God, by voice and deed.

It may be imagined that Patrick greatly needed someone to talk to about these events, to help him resolve and evaluate them. Where would a boy whose grandfather had been a priest and his father a deacon turn, but to the wise men of the Church whose teachings had once fallen so lightly upon his ears.

If, then, he found himself on that sun-drenched shelf between St Tropez and Genova, the fame of Lerinus and the brilliant and saintly men gathered there would have reached his ears. Beating his way back along the coastal road in an attempt to reach Marseilles and a passage on a ship to Britain, it requires no stretch of the imagination to picture him stopping off at Lerins to seek a sympathetic ear, instruction and comfort, and finding the peace and the company such that he remained for several years before the call of home again set his youthful feet upon the road.

But, upon this episode in his life—if it ever took place—Patrick remains completely silent.

The next words that we have from him at the conclusion

of the great adventure of escape, when at last the party encountered people and habitations once more and were saved, are brief and stark: 'And again after a few years, I was in Britain with my kin who received me as a son, and in good faith besought me that at all events now, after the great tribulations which I had undergone, I should not leave them and go elsewhere.'

Home is the wanderer, the one given up as lost for ever, boy no longer, but man, quiet, serious, changed, so different from the carefree, scatterbrained lad snatched from their midst.

Perhaps in recounting the astounding adventures that had befallen him, Patrick included the greatest of all, his finding his way to God; or perhaps this adventure of the soul the young man kept to himself. But whichever, it was over now. The storm-tossed bark had made safe anchorage. There was no need ever to put to sea again. Surrounded by his family, in good financial circumstances, Patrick was ready to assume the role for which his birth and upbringing would have prepared him: marriage, a home of his own with children, perhaps a job in the municipality, or a minor ordination such as had been taken by his father. Magonus Secatus would never have been heard from again, in this life, or any other.

But shortly after his return, as he was beginning to settle down in the bosom of his family, Patrick had a dream, which reminded him in no uncertain fashion that it was not for nothing that God had led him out of captivity and the wilderness of Hibernia. The Lord had work for him to do.

CHAPTER TWO

The Education of Patrick

I

LOOKING back two thousand years to the tragedy that took place on the Hill of Golgotha, it is perhaps difficult to understand or appreciate how near and fresh in the minds of people of the fifth century was the Passion of Christ.

A half-dozen or so generations were sufficient to bridge the gap. And in fact the men of the year 400 were closer to their ancestors of the year 1 and the Rock of Peter on which their church was founded than we are to the men of 1558. The problems of living—and dying—that concerned all humans of those times had altered little in four hundred years except to increase as the chaos attendant upon the break-up of the great peace-enforcing empire became universal. The miseries of existence that led the lowly and the downtrodden to turn to the comfort and the Kingdom promised by Jesus had multiplied. The solace of a religion that brought peace to the troubled spirit and the weary body was sorely needed. The thousand pagan years that had preceded Christianity were as nothing to the intensity or emotion with which men searched for the light and truth of God. The world was full of stories of saints and sinners who had found their way to Him, some, reaching Him by the *via dolorosa* of asceticism and self-denial in the desert, others through living fully the life of the flesh only to find it stale and wanting. God was nearer and more intelligible to the people of those days than at any time since. His voice could be heard from the mountain top; He made his wishes manifest.

Or at least, so it seemed to the fifth-century man, who gave to the Trinity of God, the Father, the Son and the Holy Spirit, a love and devotion that is difficult for modern man to comprehend.

Perhaps, too, because of this devotion the ears of the prophets, saints and apostles of the early centuries were more attuned to the voice of God than those of today. When Patrick was in Ireland as a missionary, he was often, by his own testimony, forewarned by God of dangers: 'But God is my witness,' he wrote, 'who knows all things even before they come to pass, as He used to forewarn even me, poor wretch that I am, of many things by divine message.' And again: 'And once again, after many years, I fell into captivity. On that first night I stayed with them, I heard a divine message saying to me: "Two months will you be with them." And so it came to pass: on the sixtieth night thereafter, the Lord delivered me out of their hands.'

God-words are spoken today, God is loved and praised in phrases that fall easily from the lips, but there do not appear to be the passion and the fire behind the devotion, the self-abnegation and total dedication to service that obtained in Patrick's day, or was felt and expressed by men like him.

When Patrick wrote in his *Confessio:* 'Hence, then, I give unwearied thanks to God, who kept me faithful in the day of my temptation so that today I can confidently offer Him my soul as a living sacrifice,' he meant it beyond anything that we can comprehend today, for he offered not alone his soul '. . . to Christ, my Lord, who saved me out of all my troubles,' but his body as well and his life as well, if God should wish it.

The dream or vision that came to Patrick in Britain, and which along with his conversion in Ireland was the second great turning point in his life was the following: A man whose name was Victoricus came out of Ireland bearing with him countless letters, one of which he gave to Patrick.

The Saint read the opening words of the letter which were 'The voice of the Irish,' and as he read these words it seemed to him that he heard these voices, young and old, grown men and babes, and yes, though he does not say so, perhaps the voices of the unborn as well, the unborn and unbaptised. They were the voices of those he describes as being 'beside the woods of Voclut, which is near the Western Sea . . . and thus did they cry out as with one mouth . . . "We ask thee, holy youth, come and walk among us once more." '

The call was so clear and filled with despair that Patrick broke down and wept, unable to read further and awoke.

For Voclut, read Ulaid—Dalaradia, where Patrick had been captive. And to a boy born near and brought up on the west coast of England, the Western Sea would have been that Irish Sea which washes the eastern shores of Ireland.

This was the first dream. Another night there came a second: '. . . whether within me, or beside me, I know not, God knoweth . . . they called me most unmistakably with words which I heard but could not understand, except that at the end of the prayer He spoke thus: "He that laid down His life for thee, it is He that speaketh in thee"; and so I awoke full of joy.'

You will recognise there neither a bemused nor neurotic mind, but a healthy, questioning one. Whence spoke these voices—from beside him, or *within him*? No modern analyst could ask for a more sane approach to a revelation.

And the final experience: 'And again I saw Him praying

in me, and I was as it were within my body and I heard Him
above me, that is, over the inward man and there He prayed
mightily and with groanings. And all the time I was astonished,
and wondered and thought with myself who it could be that
prayed in me. But at the end of the prayer He spoke, saying
that He was the Spirit; and so I woke up and remembered
the Apostle [Paul] saying: "The Spirit helpeth the infirmities
of our prayer. For we know not what we should pray for as
we ought; but the Spirit Himself asketh for us with unspeakable groanings which cannot be expressed in words," and
again: "The Lord our advocate asketh for us." '

It was Patrick's soul that was being summoned. Both
within and without himself, detached from his body, as it
were, an observer, almost a bystander, he was aware of the
summons and, at the end, the Summoner. From that
moment on, identifying himself with St Paul, he surrendered
himself, his career, and his life, if need be, to the task of
bringing the word of God and Christ to the heathen Irish
who had once taken him captive and with whom, but for
the intervention of that God whose prisoner he now was, he
might have spent the remainder of his days in misery and
bondage.

He was an honest man, was Patrick. A more honest one
never lived. He did not wish to go back to Ireland, to leave
his home and his family. He never seemed wholly to have
forgiven the Irish for their abduction of him. From his
eminence as a Roman citizen and a Christian, he looked
down upon them as savages and barbarians, an estimate far
from deserved. In moments of human weakness, he reminded
God as well as his superiors and critics in and beyond Britain
and Ireland of the sacrifices he had made and was making
for them. But one aspect of the Irish profoundly touched
him and continued to do so to the end of his days. They

were an unenlightened and an unbaptised people and so forbidden the paradise of heaven. He pitied them for this state; to pity is also to love.

For three centuries the Catholic Church had been seething with the problems of the human soul, free will, predestination, the whole or partial divinity of Christ and the doctrine of original sin. This latter doctrine had but recently prevailed over the Pelagian heresy of free will and sinless birth. To men of Patrick's education, beliefs and faith, the death of a person unbaptised was a greater tragedy than death itself.

Dissolution in those dark, violent ages came early, and often in horrid guise, by violence, in battle, by torture, starvation, treachery, plague, and natural cataclysms of earthquake, fire and flood. But at least it was an end, and to the believer and baptised Christian an entrance into the gates of Heaven and Paradise. But the unbaptised, the pagan, the heathen and the infidel, were doomed to limbo through and into eternity. They could not enter Heaven.

No doubt there were many who by their deeds and behaviour while on earth deserved this. But what touched the hearts of such as Patrick were the babes and infants, innocent seeming, but evil by inheritance and the mere fact of being born, who were denied redeeming baptism and eternal joy.

Some men like Pelagius tried to change the doctrine and free the just-born from this undeserved load of guilt. The men of orthodoxy who accepted the established doctrines of the Church of Rome approached the problem the hard way. They dedicated their lives to freeing the innocent and the not so innocent by conversion to belief in Christ and Baptism in His name.

The three dreams, visions or inner revelations fixed Patrick with an unwavering determination to carry the gospel to

the Irish. From that moment on he became the steadfast man
who could not be turned from his purpose.

And then once more when most we would like to accompany him along the thorny road he trod to see how he
overcame the obstacles piled in his path, to learn from
example how an indomitable will-to-achieve is not to be
turned aside, he vanishes from our ken. No more than faint
echoes of his struggles come through to us out of the past
and the welter of confused and confusing legends, surmises
and miracle tales. He himself is silent as to the years and the
manner of his preparation for his task.

The scope and magnificence of his accomplishments point
to the struggle. When St Patrick died, almost the whole of
Ireland had been Christianised and the Catholic Church
established. Christian ethics and Church Law had been made
a part of Irish law. The Latin alphabet had been introduced.
Schools and monasteries had been established and there was
already a flourishing native Irish priesthood, and a church
hierarchy and organisation along Gallo-Roman monastic
lines. There was no breath of heresy. Patrick himself had
converted and baptised thousands upon thousands of the
pagans, captured their kings and princes in his net, and won
young men and women to the celibate servitude of Christ.

So strong were the Catholicism, the faith and doctrine
that he implanted on this emerald isle that, when a century
or so after his death the final splitting asunder of the Roman
empire and the descent of the barbarian hordes brought such
confusion and darkness to the continent of Europe that it
threatened to engulf Christianity as well, it was the monks of
Ireland who dipped their torches in the flame kindled by
Patrick and brought the light back to Western Europe.

And, finally, he left upon Ireland a personal impression
that has endured for fifteen centuries. True, it is a distorted

and confused picture that has emerged from the memory
consciousness of the descendants of those who originally fell
beneath the spell of the missionary and which by now has
lost almost all traces of resemblance to the man whose personality and tongue they were unable to resist. His real
imprint lies rather in the steadfastness of the Irish to the
steadfastness of Patrick, their adherence to the faith, the Holy
Trinity that was the true love of his life. If they have lost
Patrick the man, they have never wandered from Patrick the
Apostle.

II

WHEN, where, and for how long did the Saint prepare himself for such a role? In his simplicity, Patrick credits his rise
from the mire, and whatever eminence he felt he had achieved
at the time of the writing of his *Confessio*, to God and lets in
no further light. And certainly, when one contemplates his
beginnings and his end, his life itself is in the nature of a
miracle—the laws of nature set aside for the carrying out of
God's purpose. Patrick's whereabouts from the time when
he came to his determination to answer the call from Ireland
until he once more set foot on some green slope shelving
to the sea remain still an unsolved mystery. No one yet
seems to have been able to fit all the pieces of time and place
into the puzzle.

The accepted version in the nineteenth century and early
part of the twentieth, based upon the seventh- and eighth-
century accounts of Muirchu and Tirechàn, is that Patrick
journeyed to the Continent, intending to make his way to
the Apostolic See in Rome, but paused and remained at the
church of Auxerre where he studied under the great Bishop
Germanus, that Germanus who, as reported by Bede, with

Bishop Lupus of Troyes sailed to Britain to combat the Pelagian heresy.

Raised to the Diaconate, Patrick is supposed to have spent a period of close to twenty years at Auxerre in preparation for his mission. At last, *circa* 431, it seemed his chance had come when Pope Celestine took cognizance of the scattered Christian communities in Ireland and determined to send them a Bishop. However, upon the advice of the august prelates of central France, his choice was not Patrick but Palladius, an Italian priest who had been close both to Germanus and Celestine, and Patrick appeared doomed to disappointment.

However, Palladius's mission to Ireland was accounted a failure by Muirchu, Patrick's first biographer, and he was said to have died within a year, possibly martyred. Patrick thereupon was immediately consecrated by one Bishop Amator to be a bishop, and, shortly thereafter, fortified with the blessing of the Church, much treasure in gold and silver, a staff of assistance in the form of deacons, presbyters, cooks, bodyguards, artificers, needlewomen and charioteers, set sail, full-panoplied, for the Irish coast.

This interim period is unconfirmed. Not one single scrap of written church or monastery record of him exists. Nowhere does the name of Patrick appear in the annals óf European monasteries, or any of the other names by which he was known. It is almost as though a conspiracy of silence existed against the man to whom Christianity owes so great a debt. There is also the possibility that he was never there at that time.

The story as recounted by Muirchu stands up only for the Patrician Chronology—born A.D. 385, kidnapped A.D. 400, escaped A.D. 407, returned to Britain A.D. 410, returned to Ireland A.D. 432, died March 17th A.D. 461.

But against this there is that inescapable and recurring *obit* date of *circa* A.D. 492 to which scholars, chroniclers and biographers from Muirchu down have been resolutely shutting their eyes, or attempting to explain away. If the approximate chronology and *floruit* of Patrick dating back from the A.D. 492 *obit* is correct, then the entire Auxerre-Germanus-Palladius-Amator-Pope Celestine story vanishes like smoke as though it had been nothing but a dream.

The truth would appear to be that no one can tell today with certainty or accuracy where Patrick was educated and prepared for his Irish mission, when, where and by whom ordained and later consecrated, or by whom and to what extent financed. For meagre clues and sole evidence, we must look to those documents, the *Letter*, the *Confessio*, and the fragments that bear the authentic stamp of Patrick, his character and his style.

There is, for instance, at the very beginning of the *Confessio*, and likewise scattered throughout the document, a hint that would tend to negate any long-drawn-out period of preparation extending over twenty—and as some of his early biographers have maintained, even thirty—years. It is simply that it would be impossible for any man, even one whose education had been neglected in his youth, to spend that length of time in any of the first-class ecclesiastical schools that abounded in Gaul in the early fifth century and emerge 'most unlearned,' 'ignorant,' 'unable to tell my story to those versed in the art of concise writing,' with Latin rusty and 'rustic,' unless he were a complete dunce. And every act of Patrick, even though he refers to himself as a fool, shows that he was far from being one.

What one must therefore conclude is that he was able to spend far less time in the company of, and learning from, those to whom he refers as 'men of letters on their estates

and others wise and expert in law and powerful in word'
than has been suggested, unless so lowly was his position at
whatever monastery he found himself that he was denied
schooling beyond the study of Scripture. Listen to Patrick's
ringing denunciation of the learned who at some time poured
scorn upon him:

'Wherefore, then, be astonished, ye great and little that
fear God, and you men of letters on your estates, listen and
pore over this. Who was it that roused up me, the fool that
I am, from the midst of those who in the eyes of men are
wise, and expert in law, and powerful in word and everything? And He inspired me—me the outcast of this world—
before others to be the man (if only I could!) who, with fear
and reverence without blame, should faithfully serve the
people to whom the love of Christ conveyed and gave me
for the duration of my life . . .'

No man who had been a student for twenty years at the
feet of such as Honoratus, Germanus, Amator or Lupus
could be capable of emitting such a cry of inferiority and
envy of the educated.

It is not the school, but the length of the schooling, that
seems to be ruled out. For Patrick has already placed himself
in Gaul at one period of his life, after his escape from Ireland;
it seems logical that he would return there to prepare himself for missionary work.

And it seems that again he places himself there by a longing to return at a time when his involvement with the Irish
and his duties there would no longer permit of such a visit.
For he writes: '. . . wherefor, then, even if I wished to leave
them and go to Britain—and how I would have loved to go
to my country and my parents, *and also to Gaul in order to
visit the brethren and to see the face of the Saints of my Lord* . . .'

Who were the brethren and the Saints? Surely those with

whom he was associated during a second visit there, men with whom he would have become friendly during his period of schooling and preparation of whatever duration. And it is likely that Patrick confided to one of these men the secret of the sin he had committed when he was a boy of but fifteen years and which had troubled his conscience ever since.

In the churches and monasteries of middle Gaul there was likewise to be found that staunch orthodoxy free of all taint of heresy of which Patrick partook. When the British Church at the beginning of the fifth century felt itself seriously endangered by the Pelagian heresy, it was to the Bishops of Auxerre and Troyes that they appealed for assistance in combating this peril . . .

Patrick leaves no doubt as to his orthodoxy when early in his *Confession* he states his creed:

'Because there is no other God, nor ever was, nor will be than God the Father unbegotten, without beginning, from whom all is beginning, the Lord of the universe, as we have been taught; and His son Jesus Christ, whom we declare always to have been with the Father, spiritually and ineffably begotten by the Father before the beginning of the world, before all beginning; and by Him are made all things visible and invisible. He was made man, and, having defeated death, was received into Heaven by the Father; and He hath given Him all power over all names in Heaven and on earth, and every tongue shall confess to Him that Jesus Christ is Lord and God, in whom we believe and whose advent we expect soon to be, judge of the living and of the dead, who will render to every man according to his deeds, and He has poured forth upon us abundantly the Holy Spirit, the gift and pledge of immortality, who makes those who believe and obey sons of God and joint heirs with Christ, and Him do we confess and adore, one God in the Trinity of the Holy Name.'

It would appear that, wherever the place of Patrick's preparation and whatever the situation with regard to the status of Christianity in Ireland, Patrick was regarded by his monastic colleagues as something of an eccentric with his one-track purpose of proceeding to Ireland and converting the heathen.

He reports that many opposed and tried to prevent his going on this mission, saying behind his back (and which was apparently soon enough reported to Patrick by 'friends,' indicating that neither times nor people have altered much in fifteen centuries): 'Why does this fellow throw himself into danger among enemies who have no knowledge of God?' And then Patrick adds with considerable charity: 'It was not malice, but it did not appeal to them because—and to this I own myself—of my rusticity. And I did not understand at once the grace that was then in me; now I understand that I should have done so before.'

Does a picture begin to emerge of a 'new boy,' an odd young man of some twenty-seven to thirty years, perhaps, a foreigner, one of those blue-eyed Britons from across the Channel appearing in the midst of learned men and book scholars whose lives have been dedicated to the Church from childhood on and whose early training had been initiated with this in mind?

This fellow who could at first speak no French, whose Latin was distinctly 'provincial,' what there was of it, believed that he was divinely inspired to spend his life bringing the gospel to a nation of savages so far beyond the pale on their island out there in the Western Ocean that they had not even been brought into the Roman orbit.

If they knew about Patrick's Irish adventure, his familiarity with the people, their customs and their language, it was probably counted against him and was considered a part of his eccentricity. To the bookish, the qualifications for advancement are to be found only in books.

Patrick had one great chink in his armour. Strong-willed, stubborn, courageous, completely unconcerned for his own life, comfort or safety, steadfast and unyielding of purpose, he yet cared greatly what people said. The main purpose of the writing of the *Confessio* was that it should serve as an answer to his critics in Gaul, in Britain, and in Ireland itself.

It would seem that Patrick was aware of this weakness. Not realising at once that he was something special, or because the memory of his dreams had dimmed, or he had been shamed by the comments of his companions, he may have been constrained to let them mock him out of pressing more immediately for what he wished. In his old age, looking back upon his career and seeing how God had aided him at every turn, how indeed he seemed to have been selected for this work, he understands that he should have realised this earlier during this period of preparation and that perhaps some precious time might have been lost by letting himself be put out by monastery gossip, and the instincts of the herd to turn upon and be hostile to the individual—the man who by birth, speech or force of character is 'different.'

The opposition of his fellows and superiors did not prevail, for eventually, still unlearned, still rustic, Patrick found his way to Ireland and his life's work.

It is possible that he was no more than a simple ordained priest when first he came to Ireland. Perhaps he was not elected and consecrated a bishop until his apostleship to the Irish had begun to bear such fruit that his superiors on the mainland could no longer ignore either him or his work.

And even then, he charges bitterly, he was attacked by a

number of his seniors who brought up his sins against his laborious episcopate: 'On that day indeed was I struck so that I might have fallen now and for eternity; but the Lord graciously spared the stranger and sojourner for His name and came mightily to my help in this affliction. Verily, not slight was the shame and blame that fell upon me! I ask God that it may not be reckoned to them as a sin.

'As cause for proceeding against me they found, after thirty years, a confession I had made before I was a Deacon. In the anxiety of my troubled mind I confided to my dearest friend what I had done one day, nay, in one hour because I was not yet strong. I know not, God knoweth whether I was then fifteen years old and I did not believe in the living God.'

The proceedings, whatever they were—a synod gathered to consider Patrick's elevation to bishop, or constituted to hear charges against him brought by those envious of his astonishing and unexpected success in Ireland—were apparently held in Britain with Patrick absent in Ireland and brought forth the bitterest disillusionment of Patrick's life. He heard, believed, or was led to believe that his best friend had betrayed his confidence.

There is a possible clue to the source of Patrick's finances in Ireland, and it is to be found in a paragraph of Patrick's fiery letter to Coroticus.

Referring once more to the sacrifices he has made, Patrick writes: 'I was freeborn according to the flesh. I am the son of a Decurion. *But I sold my noble rank*—I am neither ashamed or sorry—for the good of others. Thus I am a servant of Christ to a foreign nation for the unspeakable glory of life everlasting which is in Christ Jesus, our Lord.'

Did Patrick underwrite his own mission from the proceeds of the sale of his patent of nobility? Did he after the death of his father pledge his patrimony and devote his share of the inheritance as well as his title in the interest of the Irish mission when his superiors remained still doubtful as to his fitness and reluctant to back him with funds? He would not have been the first saint to have disposed of all his worldly goods for the greater glory of God.

III

SOME of the details of Patrick's education and preparation for his missionary work may be gleaned both from his own two documents and the various 'Lives' written of him.

The large retinue with which at one time he travelled in Ireland, as given by *The Tripartite Life* and listed elsewhere in this book, and the material and properties he needed to carry with him to establish his churches on the orthodox Gallic lines appear to be corroborated by himself, when he tells how through the treachery of princelings, already paid off as guides and protectors through doubtful territory, he and his companions were captured and their equipment— 'everything they found with us'—taken away.

Thus there were companions and there was gear. Somewhere Patrick had to become familiar with the organisation and duties of his retinue and the use of the various items connected with church ritual.

It may be that his train was peculiarly Irish and adapted to Irish customs and culture and that the Saint learned as he went along, in that country.

For instance, if the retinue listed in *The Tripartite Life* is correct and Patrick included a cowherd in his entourage, one would not expect to find the same in the party of a missionary, say, to the heathen Franks of Clovis or other pagans who might have some kind of monetary system or a different standard of value. Patrick's cowherd was really the

cashier of his bank and here we have an adaptation to local
custom, since in Ireland the cow was the standard of value,
interchangeable with an ounce of gold.

The founding of a church in Ireland in Patrick's time
meant not only providing the congregation by converting
and baptising the inhabitants of a district and a clergy by
training and ordaining native priests, but raising the edifice
that would contain them and act as a place of worship.
Patrick not only founded churches; he and his companions
had to build them, for, with the exception of Dichu's barn
which Patrick converted and consecrated, there were no
buildings in ancient Ireland intended for worship. Celtic
theology was an outdoors affair.

But again local custom and material came into the picture,
and Patrick could not have learned how to build an Irish
church at Lerinus or Auxerre or elsewhere in southern
France, if that is where he was at school. People use the
material of the land in which they live. The Romans built
with great blocks of *tufa* and brickwork, the Greeks with
marble, others with stone. The Irish used that which was
the easiest for them to handle and of which there was an
abundance, namely wood. And for even quicker and simpler
construction they availed themselves of wattles, or reeds,
interwoven, with the interstices rain- and wind-proofed by
daubing with clay.

All the Patrician churches were built either of timber, or
clay and wattles, which of course is why none of them has
survived. But, again, the construction of these buildings
called for a skill that the Saint must have acquired in Ireland,
either as a boy slave when he might have been summoned
to aid his master in erecting a new byre, or later upon his
return with native builders and artisans in his retinue. It is
also possible that, when Patrick had acquired a piece of land

suitable for a church and permission to build, he engaged native local labour familiar with the erection of buildings in that part of the country, and no doubt pitching in and lending a hand himself.

However, the making of altars, altar cloths, chalices, patens and all other necessary Catholic ecclesiastical essentials was an imported art, since no such articles existed in Ireland before the coming of the Christians though there is one interesting tale told of Patrick on one of his trips being led to a cave where were concealed four chalices, indicating that there were Christian rites already performed before his coming. Until native workers were trained to these, all the furnishings of Patrick's early churches must have been the result of foreign imported craftsmen, both women and men. Knowledge of what was required Patrick must have come by on the mainland, or in Great Britain. If, indeed, he financed himself in his early years and went to Ireland from Britain, it is not beyond the bounds of possibility that members of his own family, including females, accompanied him in the capacity of sewers and embroiderers, along with their families, giving rise to the many stories of Patrick's sisters and nephews being in Ireland with him.

Somewhere Patrick had to acquire the practical side of Church foundation and missionary work and, since the idea of devoting his life to the conversion of the heathen Irish did not occure to Patrick until the visions or dreams that took place after his return to Britain from Gaul and the Isles of the Tyrrhene Sea, it must have been at the time of his second visit to Gaul.

But as to when and where, we have no certain clue. We know only that Patrick was able to do all that was necessary in the foundation, building, furnishing and staffing of a church.

Perhaps he picked it up merely by observation. For there seems little indication that the Gallic monasteries and ecclesiastical schools of his day were organised to teach and specifically train missionaries to foreign lands as do the schools today, where the young man is made not only into priest, but a little of doctor, chemist, biologist, sanitary engineer and schoolmaster as well, so that he may be all things to his primitive flock and be prepared to cope with almost any contingency.

Some such training centres may have existed in early Christian Gaul, but history seems to indicate that the concern, for instance, of so great and important a prelate as Germanus, Bishop of Auxerre, lay in the theological field, and he is celebrated by Bede mainly for rescuing the British Church from the Pelagian and other heresies.

Palladius, the first to be sent by Pope Celestine to function as Bishop to the Scots (Irish) believing in Christ, appears to have been priest, theologian, politician and church official, but the period of his residence in Ireland is obscure and there is no real indication that he was an efficient and effective missionary in the sense that Patrick was. The pious and holy St Patrick was a practical man who could get things done, or do them himself.

Yet the indications from Patrick's own words are that the school in Gaul, or the monastery where he went to prepare himself of his life's work in Ireland, was pedantic rather than practical, for the other scholors there made fun of him for his rusticity, that is his un-learning, and were critical that one so lacking should wish to throw himself into danger amongst enemies who had no knowledge of God, etc. Patrick had everything else: zeal, a first-hand knowledge of the Irish and their language, and organisational skill, proficiences that would have counted heavily in his favour in any college preparing a man for foreign service.

Patrick knew his Bible as few men have, from cover to cover, both the Old and the New Testament. In the two brief documents that have come down to us from his hand, the *Confession* and the *Letter*, there are quotations from 23 out of the 27 books of the New Testament, as well as from 15 of the books of the Old Testament and Apocrypha.

Scholars such as Prof. Ludwig Bieler and the Rev. Newport J. D. White have pointed out that Patrick was not a one-book man either, but that his writings show evidence of familiarity with the works of St Cyprian, Augustine, Victorinus of Pettau, the Latin Irenaeus and perhaps one or two contemporary Church writers. These scholars have also suggested that the version of the Bible that he used was the one in vogue in the southern part of Gaul during his era.

In all the welter of legend and miracle-working that has grown up about Patrick it has been generally overlooked by those attempting to round out a portrait of this unique man that he was one of the most competent of church lawyers of his times and thoroughly familiar with the ecclesiastical legislation of the era.

The man who ventures into the dangers of the unknown, unarmed, in the pursuit of a faith and an ideal is a romantic figure, and this romance of physical courage, gallantry and spiritual strength surrounds Patrick as it does the great soldier who is victorious in battle. But the Saint went a step farther than the general. He cemented his own victories through his knowledge of Church law and his ability to organise his foundations along practical lines, legally. He spread the network of his legal system over Ireland one that functioned parallel to the Irish Code, until at some stage of the Christianisation of Ireland, High Bishop and High

King and an assemblage of clerics and lawyers managed to
weave together, or link up wherever possible, the two sets
of laws and definitely allocate and limit the jurisdiction of
church and state. How much more manly and noble this
work than some of the childish acts ascribed to Patrick by
his earlier biographers.

Muirchu, whose *Life of Patrick* was written in about the
year 688, extricates himself neatly from the criticism of his
own and succeeding centuries by referring in his introduction
to the burden of the task of story-telling laid upon him by
his superior, Bishop Aedh, because of conflicting opinions
and the very many surmises of very many persons, and
adds: 'My skill is small; my authorities are uncertain [or]
anonymous; my memory is treacherous etc. etc.' Already
then they were guessing about Patrick.

Patrick is done no discredit in Muirchu's account of how
he bore the disappointment of seeing Palladius appointed
in his stead to go to Ireland, for the evidence of the Saint's
own writing shows him to have been humble and able to
accept adversity of any kind beyond his own powers to
mend as the verdict of God. But from there on the story
becomes too fictionally pat—the convenient failure of
Palladius and his fading from the picture (which might have
had some historical basis) and Patrick there as the scorned
understudy ready to step into his shoes and make good, like
any ambitious fill-in waiting for his prima donna or star to
collapse.

There is equal drama, perhaps even more, in the other
possible story of the zealous missionary priest, passed over
by his superiors, believing in his modesty that their scorn
and strictures were deserved, but at last recognising himself
as prepared for the venture and taking the bit between his
teeth.

No longer a callow youth, but a rounded man who, if weak in rhetoric, was strong in all else, and particularly in the faith that God had chosen him for this work, he could have returned to Ireland and, with the sale of his patrimony and the conscripting of members of his own family, embarked for Ireland to devote the proceeds of that sale to the Christian charity of saving from hellfire eternal the souls of those who once had deprived him of his freedom.

Even more than the other story—if such was Patrick's introduction to Ireland—it points up sharply the nature of this man who, once the way and the need was made clear to him, never once wavered in his service to God or the Irish.

CHAPTER THREE

Patrick in Ireland

I

IRELAND today is a beautiful and mournful land in which dwell the remnants of a once great, cultured and noble race. It is a country and a people that has been savaged, ravished and betrayed as have few other nations. Fate and the march of history seem to have been at particular pains to leave the Irish little beyond the pride of memory, their poets and the poetry of their legends. All other evidence of the advance of Irish civilisation in pre-Christian and Christian times has been destroyed and there remains nothing but a few barrows, stone circles, a canoe or a bronze sword, or a golden torque dug out of some bog.

They built of wood, clay and wattles on shifting sands; except for a few Ogham inscriptions on stones and the secret rolls of the Druids, they wrote not at all. But their code of law was as enlightened as the Roman's, and their respect for an obedience to it strict. Their sagas and bardic literature soared higher and more imaginatively than anything similiar produced in the Roman world. The Greek and the Roman civilisations produced great poets from time to time, but the Irish were a race and a nation of poets. Poetry and a love and understanding for it beat in the lowliest and most humble heart. The bards sang and narrated the glories of the past, the present and the future not to a class, but to one and all. The Irish found poetry in war, in love, in nature, in the sun, moon and stars and the wind and rains, in the sea, the naked moors and the great forest lands and mountains and in all living things. It was probably for this reason that Christianity appealed to them, for Patrick appeared amongst them and preached them a poem of a loving and forgiving God, and told them a moving and poetic story of the conception, birth, death and resurrection of His only begotten son.

The Irish of the fifth century were a gay, life-loving people who could be bemused by a beautiful woman, a fine horse, the exquisite action of a running deer, or the death of a brave man pierced by a multitude of swords but still resolutely facing the enemy—one who would be buried with all his weapons, standing up and *still* facing towards the foe.

They were vital, virile, often brutal; they slaughtered one another gaily in sectional wars, stole one another's cattle and women, drank and feasted, wore fine clothes and magnificent gold bracelets, necklaces and brooches when they could afford it and in general played the male and human devil over their beautiful, green, wooded country.

Their theology was simple, nature and object or idol-worship, or rather respect for nature's great signposts to God, the sun, the moon and the stars overhead. It required no priesthood. The Druids were never priests, but interpreters, prophets, teachers, magicians, lawyers, judges, bards and poets. They were the keepers of the Irish soul until Patrick came along and showed them how that soul might be blended and united with that God who had created all the beauty in and about them.

It takes two to consummate a conversion. If Patrick was persuasive—and no more earnest, determined and silver-tongued apostle ever carried the Gospel to the Heathen—

then the Irish must also have had the ears with which to hear
him. To abandon Paganism, in thought, at least, and in one
generation to accept the word of Jesus, as did the Irish,
bespeaks not only the character of a great missionary to carry
the Divine Word, but also a race or nation of poets, dreamers
and warm-hearted, understanding men.

The Irish, it seemed, were peculiarly receptive to
Christianity. It fitted their natures like another skin and,
over fifteen centuries, their devotion to it has remained
unchanged. More, they were receptive to Catholicism and
the Catholic Church, the teachings and preachings of Patrick;
and, except for the small, north-western corner of Ulster
which is Protestant, they have retained roughly the same
Catholicism as that which they learned at Patrick's feet.
Betrayal, robbery, slaughter, persecution, deportations,
wars, revolutions and famine have had no effect upon the
Catholicism of the survivors. Never was a sturdier vine
planted in a more receptive soil.

One of the most astonishing facets of Patrick as self-
revealed in the two documents he left behind him, the human
Confessio and the angry and majestic *Letter*, is that the Saint
appeared to be utterly unaware of this child-like and poetic
side of the 'savages,' 'heathen' and 'barbarians' whose Apostle,
protector and Saint he became.

Perhaps when you have been beaten over the head by a
horde of wild and hairy men, hustled into an evil-smelling
craft and sailed away from kith and kin across the sea and
into forced labour as a slave, it becomes somewhat difficult
to see them as fun-loving children with better natures aspiring
to beauty.

Yet deep down, somewhere inside him, perhaps buried in
the unconscious, he must have loved them, or loved some
side of them, for when in the vision they called to him to

come and walk in their midst once more, he set aside self, family, luxury, ease and comfort and devoted himself to the end of his days to their service.

There is no doubt about the Irish—those whom he converted—loving him. Those that did not love him respected him as that steadfast and unchanging man whose word was his bond, who never lied, never shirked a task no matter how dangerous or onerous it might be, and, unarmed, could look death in the face with the same fearless equanimity demonstrated by any Irish hero warrior. If the Irish as a people did not appeal to St Patrick, he most certainly appealed to them. They often tried to kill but never to belittle him. He established the stature of his personality and the extraordinary power of his faith from the moment he set foot once more upon Irish soil, and it never diminished.

II

IF Patrick in his *Confessio* is exasperatingly silent as to when and where he trained and when, where and how he came to Ireland, he is even more so in what he is content to reveal about his life's work in Ireland, a mission which lasted at the very least 28 years and may have extended even over a period of 40 years.

No man ever summed up a life that was to become a part of the history of the soul more modestly, or in fewer words: 'Now it would be tedious to give a detailed account of all my labours or even a part of them. Let me tell you briefly how the merciful God often freed me from slavery and from twelve dangers in which my life was at stake—not to mention numerous plots, which I cannot express in words; for I do not wish to bore my readers.'

There must have been many more of such plots and dangers

in a country in which clever Druid lawyers and advisers-about-the-throne would be quick to point out the political dangers of yielding to a religion which acknowledged God and not man as the King and whose ethics were, to say the least, somewhat constricting to a freebooting monarch.

The danger period must have been those early times of Patrick's mission before the Druids learned that by embracing Christianity they could not only retain their positions as teachers, prophets and counsellors, but to this could also add sacerdotal powers, powers that were far more effective in their control over the masses than their somewhat doubtful magical potency. Once the Druids had accepted the truth of the slogan, 'If you can't lick 'em, join 'em,' Patrick's greatest dangers must have been over.

'All the while,' wrote Patrick, as we have seen, 'I used to give presents to the kings besides the fees I paid to their sons who travel with me,' and then gives us a glimpse of an instance where this policy went wrong: 'Even so they laid hands on me and my companions and on that day they eagerly wished to kill me; but my time had not yet come. And everything they found with us they took away, and they put me in irons; and on the fourteenth day, the Lord delivered me from their power; and our belongings were returned to us because of God and our dear friends whom we had seen before.'

To this class of incident and danger must be added that other experience related in a paragraph of the *Confessio* which is mysteriously misplaced in Patrick's early narrative, as though by association it had suddenly occurred to him, and he, being no writer conscious of the dictates of form and continuity, simply put it down at that point.

'And once again, after many years, I fell into captivity. On that first night I stayed with them, I heard a divine

C

message, the answer of God, saying to me: "For two months thou shalt be with them." And so it came to pass. On the sixtieth night thereafter, the Lord delivered me out of their hands.'

Into these incidents we may read not only something of the methods of Patrick, but also of his enemies. They were not savages or barbarian brutes, but reasonable men with a political sense who found themselves with a problem on their hands. When they possessed themselves physically of the core of the problem, namely the person of Patrick, they seemed to have sought reasonably for a solution instead of blindly butchering him out of hand, as might have been the case had they been Communists, Nazis, or Red Indians on the warpath.

The party for immediate liquidation, one of the most workable and oft used political expedients, put forth its claims: '. . . and on that day they eagerly wished to kill me'; the moderation party counselled otherwise, since it was known that Patrick had powerful friends who might resent his passing to the point where Patrick dead could become even more of a problem to them than Patrick alive—and the fortunate good sense of the moderation party prevailed: '. . . but my time had not yet come.'

Other indications are likewise deducible. Whatever might have been the period of Patrick's career when the incident occurred, he seemed to have been travelling in retinue, as told in *The Tripartite Life*, for 'companions' were seized as well as Patrick and all their gear—'everything they found with us'—which must have been ecclesiastical and of value, consisting of metal, such as iron and bronze for the making of bells, altars, chalices, and cloth and linen and embroidery thread for the making of altar cloths, book covers and vestments, a rich haul.

A list of Patrick's retinue appears as follows in *The Tripartite Life*, a collection of biographical material, part fancy, part derived from sources now lost to us, compiled in the middle of the tenth or beginning of the eleventh century:

'These are the four and twenty persons who were said to be in orders with Patrick, namely:

Sechnal his Bishop

Mochta his priest

Bishop Macc Cairthinn his champion

Benén his psalmist

Coeman of Cell Riada his chamberlain

Sinell of Cell-Dareis his bell-ringer

Athcen of Both Domnaig his cook

Presbyter Mescan of Domnach Mescain at Fochain, his brewer

Presbyter Bescna of Domnach Dala his chaplain

Presbyter Catan and Presbyter Acan his two waiters

Odran of Disert Odrain in Hui-Failgi his charioteer

Presbyter Manach his firewood man

Rottan his cowherd

His three smiths, namely Macc-Cecht, Laeban of Domnach Laeban (it is he that made the bell called Findfaidech) and Fortchern in Rath Adine

Essa and Bite and Tassach his three artisans

His three embroideresses namely Lupait and Erc, daughter of Daire, and Cruimthiris in Cengoba

'And that is the number that should be in Joseph's company, and it is the number that should be at the King of Cashel's table down from the times of Feidlimed, son of Crimthann, King of the two provinces of Munster, etc.'

Though the list may be suspect it is at the same time interesting in its presentation of the kind of train with which Patrick might well have travelled. The foundation of an

Irish church was physical as well as spiritual labour. Macc Cairthinn, the champion, Patrick's strong man and body-guard, is encountered throughout Patrick's legend and pseudo-biography, a curious appendage for a peaceful bishop and one more suited to a king since it was Patrick's point that he needed no protector or champion but God. How-ever, the chief duty of strong-man Macc Cairthinn seemed to have been to lift Patrick aloft in his brawny arms when they came to a ford in a river that had to be negotiated and carry him across dry-shod. The Saint did not like to get his feet wet.

III

THERE were no cities in Ireland in Patrick's time. The country was divided into five major areas and these were subdivided into smaller states or *Tuatha*, each independently ruled by a chieftain or king, who yielded some degree of authority to the King of one of the five greater divisions, who in turn were in a measure subject to one High King who was based in Tara in Meath.

However, these hierarchical connections were not feudal, but legal. Each chief or kinglet maintained his complete independence, looked after his own subjects, warred with whom he pleased and acted in accordance with his own interests. But the laws of Ireland were not restricted to family, or tribe, or petty kingdom, to be changed or ad-ministered at the whim or will of the local chieftain. They embraced the whole of the country and all the Tuatha and states were subject to them. And the Druids were the formu-lators, advocates, recorders and keepers of the law. Ireland might have been likened to a number of independent cor-porations operating under the shelter of one corporate name and of which the High King was chairman of the board and conducted the meetings when the corporation chiefs gathered upon occasions at board meetings to discuss matters common and of interest to them all.

As an example of the power or non-power of the High King, had he succumbed to Patrick's preaching and embraced Christianity—which, incidentally, he apparently did not— he could not have forced or ordered kings or chieftains of any regions outside his own to do likewise. In other words, he could not have made Christianity the state religion as had Rome. He could give his approval to Patrick preaching and converting in his own territory—which he seems to have done—but this licence was of no value beyond the boundaries of that territory except for the prestige accruing to Patrick through such permission and evidence of friendship and approval.

But had Patrick been murdered anywhere in Ireland, it would have been a matter for the High King to see that justice was done and the murderers brought to book.

It seems not too far-fetched to suspect from Patrick's own words that he had some kind of intelligence-network operating for him once he had established himself and his mission in Ireland.

Patrick is captured by some petty king to whom he has already made gifts, betrayed by the king's son who is already on his pay-roll. The Saint is manacled, his companions bound, and all their equipment and property seized. For two days it is touch and go while the debate rages whether it is worth the risk to kill this man whose presence and message are upsetting all the established notions.

But in the meantime, a messenger is streaking through the forest—a member of the company who had escaped in the confusion of the ambuscade, or some young princeling whose devotion to the Apostle transcended that of convert to priest and had waxed to that of son and father. The message 'Patrick has been taken! They may kill him!' is sufficient tocsin to rally and inflame friends of Patrick in neighbouring Tuatha. Arms are snatched up, horses harnessed to chariot poles. Then, one night from the outskirts of the Dun or Palace fortress where Patrick lies, an owl hoots and is answered by another; followed a shout and the iron clangour of sword, spear and shield and the Dun is overwhelmed and Patrick is safe. He and his men are freed. His property, the property of his church is restored to him by 'dear friends whom we had seen before.' Another translation of this passage in the *Confession* is: '. . . and whatever was ours was restored to us for the sake of God and the near friends whom we had provided beforehand.'

A reasonable modernisation might also be: '. . . I am not sure of these people into whose territory I am proceeding. Nevertheless I must go, and unarmed and unguarded. However, if you do not hear from me within a certain time . . .'

We have seen Patrick refer to his expenditures: 'You know how much I paid those who administered justice in all those districts to which I came frequently. I think I distributed not less than the price of fifteen men . . .'

These judges were kings or chieftains of Tuatha or even groups of such small territories. Patrick was a preacher, an apostle, a visionary, a dreamer of dreams, but he was also no fool. When persuasion failed to make an impression upon a chief or kinglet, he bought him.

If you find this astonishing or are inclined to be shocked, you must remember that Patrick was a man of steadfast and unchanging purpose and that his mind and energies were, from the day of a certain dream, fixed upon that purpose. To find a saint himself confessing, without excuse or embarrassment, to an act of bribery and merely saying to his critics 'you know how much I spent and what I spent it for' really removes all element of bribery or suborning from the affair and makes it no more than the customary thing to do at the time and place.

The amount invested, incidentally—the 'price of fifteen men'—seems surprisingly small. There was no currency in Ireland in the fifth century. The general standard of value was a full-grown ox or cow, which was equal in worth to one ounce of gold. Humans then became a medium of exchange as well, when it was generally recognised that a slave girl had the value of three cows. Apparently the male slave was considered of less worth, a single cow. St Finnen wished to purchase the freedom of a certain slave from a chief. The price named for him was an ounce of gold. Finnen gave the chief a gold ring of exactly that weight.

The price of fifteen men then distributed by Patrick to local chieftains would have been fifteen cows, or the equivalent of fifteen ounces of gold. Whether Patrick was using funds of the Catholic Church supplied from the mainland or his own money, he was achieving results—converts by the thousands and the spread of Christianity over all Ireland.

Patrick was and remained sensitive about his lack of book learning to the end of his days because his work brought him into contact with so many scholars and learned men. But even a casual perusal of his two documents—when allowance is made for the fashion of self-denigration of the clergy of that era—reveals that he was no fool and knew what he knew. And that which he knew best, besides the thunder of the Scriptures, was the Irish.

Scatterbrained boy or no, when he was kidnapped by the Irish at the age of sixteen, Patrick used his eyes and ears to good purpose during the six years of his slavery in Dalaradia.

He had the intelligence to note that the seat of power lay not with the people but with the chieftains or kings, and that the source of power was land. There were three equally important classes amongst the freemen of the Tuatha: the property owner; the professional men, which included the Druids; and the craftsmen. These three classes were enfranchised and its members as citizens had an equal voice in the councils. But of these, the man of property wielded the most political power, and the king as the largest property owner, as well as judge and military leader and chairman of the assemblies, held just about all the skeins of power knotted in one fist.

Patrick observed this, or acquired the knowledge by osmosis. He never made the mistake of appealing to the Irish people over the heads of their kings for he knew it would have been fruitless. Churches cannot be built upon air. Their foundations must be dug into the ground. The man with the greatest amount of disposable land was the king. Throughout all the Lives and legends of Patrick, you will find him begging, arguing, wheedling and coaxing a bit of land out of a monarch for the building of his church, such as when he asked Daire for the bit of high ground at Armagh, but had to be content with a lower parcel until his example of unchanging steadfastness and disdain for material gain for himself won him the King's admiration . . . and the piece of hilltop.

Unarmed men of peace living in communities dedicated to war and violence often need protection. The king, as military leader—and, in a sense, police chief as well—was the man to provide this.

And as the executor of the laws and chairman of all of the councils that made, changed or amended the laws, the king was the power to which Patrick must turn when the time came to bring the laws of man and the laws of God and Church into conformity.

Patrick's success in the conversion of the Irish was almost as great a political as a spiritual and emotional achievement. He had failures, as with King Laoghaire of Tara, the High King, who remained a pagan to the end of his day and was buried upright with his weapons, facing the enemy; but Patrick *made no mistakes*. If he could not convert a king, he converted their wives and sons and daughters. Those whom he could not convert he often persuaded to permit him to preach in their territory and even to establish churches there. Those whom he could not persuade, he bought for whatever was their price. It was after these necessary formalities were concluded that he went forth and pierced the hearts of the people with his eloquence and fervour and harvested their souls by the thousands.

IV

WHETHER or not Patrick came to Ireland as a bishop, or a simple missionary priest, Bishop he was at the time he wrote his *Confessio* and the *Letter to the Soldiers of Coroticus*. Of this there can be no doubt, for in the latter he declares so himself, beginning: 'I, Patrick, a sinner, unlearned, resident in Ireland, declare myself to be a bishop. Most assuredly, I believe that what I am I have received from God.'

Some attempt has been made to force the interpretation upon the above that Patrick was self-appointed and self-ordained. It will not stand up. Every line written by Patrick, every known act of his breathes respect for law, both church and civil—what is right, what is wrong, what is permissible, what is not. In the 'Book of Armagh,' which contains copies of both the *Letter* and the *Confession*, there is a fragment of considerable historical value: 'Caetiacus and Sacellus ordained bishops, priests, deacons and other clerics without consulting Patrick in Mag Ai. And Patrick accused them and sent a letter to them, and in repentance they went out to Armagh to Patrick and did the penance of monks, two willing boys of Patrick. And he said to them "Your churches will not be big." '—in other words their parishes and jurisdiction were reduced as further punishment.

Such a man would not have been self-appointed. There can be no question but that Patrick was a regularly ordained bishop with the whole weight and authority of the Catholic Church with the Pope at its head behind him, in spite of criticism levelled at him. There has never been any man of eminence, lay or clerical, who has not drawn critical fire at some time or other or been the target of the envious. If the above fragment is acceptable in its entirety, the indications are that not only was Patrick a bishop, but he was the bishop in authority in Ireland, in power an archbishop, a rank in the church hierarchy not yet established in those days.

Likewise his own testimony would seem to bear this out in the lines from the *Confessio:* 'But I see myself exalted even in the present world beyond measure by the Lord, and I was not worthy nor such that He should grant me this.' Also it is obvious that neither Patrick nor any churchman would have dared to ordain clergy and consecrate bishops had he himself not been regularly consecrated.

The *Confessio* is filled with references to the ordination of clergy everywhere by Patrick—'for a people just coming to the faith.'

It is not difficult to see that one of his gravest problems in Ireland was the result of his early success. The number of converts quickly outstripped the supply of available clergy to look after their needs. That Patrick was able to cope successfully with this situation gives a further clue to the character of the man and his talent for organisation. He gives us an oblique clue to the existence of this organisation in his paraphrase of Jesus's 'Come ye after me and I will make ye fishers of men' (Matt. 4:19; Mark 1:17), where he writes: 'Hence it was most necessary to spread our nets so that a great multitude and throng might be caught for God and that there be clerics everywhere to baptise and exhort a people in need and want.'

Thus Patrick went about Ireland not only preaching, exhorting, converting, baptising, politicking, founding churches, but he simultaneously selected, educated and trained a native clergy to staff these churches.

Like all self-made men, he made up for his lack of education in shrewdness and acumen. He selected his students from amongst the most intelligent of the strata in Ireland, the young princes, sons of kings and chieftains, and their teachers, the Druids, bards and Brehons, the poets and intelligentsia of the country.

The phrase from the fragment from the Book of Armagh, quoted above, '. . . two willing boys of St Patrick,' has been taken as an indication confirmed by some of the Lives that in addition to adults studying with him for ordination, Patrick had a school of youths filled with princelings or other bright selected boys who showed themselves as material suitable for training for the Irish clergy.

So much schooling, hasty and primitive though it may have been in the beginning and expanding hugely later, called for a knowledge of reading and writing, and art once reserved to the Druids, but now, owing to the necessity of organising a large priesthood, a gift to be made available to the many. Patrick introduced the Latin alphabet and language into Ireland, spread it wherever he went or paused, and brought to Ireland the key to universal education, thus for ever ending the isolation of that country and nation from the Continent, and forging therewith what were to become indissoluble ties with Rome and the Roman church.

Other things, the *Confession* reveals, were introduced by Patrick into Ireland, to which, one may confess with some astonishment, the early Irish took with enthusiasm—the monastic ideal and life and sexual continence practised not only by monks and 'virgins of Christ' and married clergy, but in a number of instances by civilian couples as well.

The morals of the Irish of the late pre-Christian were no worse than those of the Continent and probably even better; divorce was a simple matter, concubinage existed, and female slaves were there to be used ruthlessly and cruelly by their owners.

War and the deeds of heroes appeared to be the prime subjects of Irish legendary poetry, but love was not far behind; the women involved in the hero tales are always the most beautiful upon whom the sun ever shone and there is a healthy lustiness indicated in the relationship between the sexes. Yet, in a single generation, Patrick changed all this—at least among his Christian converts—and imposed a moral code which apparently suited the Irish temperament better than their former habits, or perhaps in some manner that we do not know it might even have resembled it, for it has lasted until this day.

'The sons and daughters of the kings of the Irish are seen to be monks and virgins of Christ,' writes Patrick. 'Among others, a blessed Irishwoman of noble birth, beautiful, adult, whom I baptised, came to us after a few days for a particular reason: she told us that she had received a message from an angel of God and he admonished her to be a virgin of Christ and draw near to God. Thanks be to God, on the sixth day after this she most laudably and eagerly chose what all virgins of Christ do. Not that their fathers agree with them; no, they often even suffer persecution and undeserved reproaches from their parents; and yet their number is ever increasing. How many have been reborn there so as to be of our kind, I do not know—not to mention widows and those who practise continence.'

'. . . *so as to be of our kind.*' Here, as well as elsewhere as will be gone into later, Patrick reveals his own chastity and continence while in Ireland.

The Saint continues on this subject: 'But greatest is the suffering of those women who live in slavery. All the time they have to endure terror and threats. But the Lord gave His grace to many of His maidens; for though they are forbidden to do so, they follow Him bravely.'

It is not quite clear from this last whether Irish female slaves in Patrick's time were forbidden to embrace Christianity and become converts, or whether the stricture was merely against their right to deny their bodies to their masters. But of Patrick's concern for them and this particular phase of their servitude there is no doubt whatsoever. His greatest concern after the fatal raid upon his converts by the pirates of Coroticus was not so much for the baptised dead who were assured of entrance into Paradise, or the valuables lost in the onslaught, but for the baptised women who had been taken to be sold into the brothels of Europe. In the close of this angry epistle he hopes that God will inspire the aggressors to recover their senses, repent their heinous murders of brethren of the Lord, but, above all, release the baptised women whom they took captive . . . 'in order that they may deserve to live to God, and be made whole here and in eternity!'

In spite of his phenomenal success in gaining converts, and

the strength of his organisation, Patrick never felt secure in Ireland—secure, that is, in the stability of his churches or even, for that matter, of the Pagans whom he had baptised. Twice does he in his *Confessio* refer to the possibility of backsliding should he abandon his flock. In one of these revealing moments he is sighing for his native land and his family there, as well as his friends in France. Yet he cannot give in to this desire, for he is bound by the Spirit which gives evidence against him, his conscience, 'telling me that I shall be guilty; and I am afraid of losing the labour which I have begun.' And again he writes: 'Wherefore may God never permit it to happen to me that I should lose His people which He purchased in the utmost parts of the world.'

It was probably the very nature of the Church he had established—Catholic, but staffed with ex-pagans—that Patrick feared, for he knew his Irish. He need not have done so. It is true the Church did alter its character somewhat after his death, but the ties with Rome that Patrick forged were never dissolved and even though the parent church on the mainland was content to let the Irish go their own free individual way, that country has remained one of the most unswervingly Catholic of all, and faithful to Rome to this day.

But one curious revenge the Druids-turned-priest had upon Patrick after his death. When they came to write his biography, or collect anecdota about him some two hundred years after his passing, they turned this good, pious man of consummate constancy, touching sensitivity and personal insecurity into a spiteful and vindictive Druid magician.

V

THE number of Irish personally baptised by Patrick during his years in Ireland is hardly to be estimated. In the *Letter*,

Patrick declares he cannot count the number of sons and daughters of kings persuaded by him to become monks and virgins of Christ, and in another passage he refers to fair and beloved brethren and sons whom he has begotten in Christ, countless of number.

Twice in the *Confessio*, he refers to the baptised as so many thousands of people. Rites of purification have always had an appeal to the primitive. Avoidance of pollution and polluting substances, and cleansing after pollution have been man's occupation and concern since the earliest times. The foreign priest with the shaven head and the commanding eyes, who spoke Irish like a native and with an eloquence and faith that could charm the birds out of the trees, preached that man entered this world already polluted by an ancient sin, but that belief in his God and the sprinkling of clear water from a meadow-well cleansed man of this stain, freed him from the bondage of Hell in the Hereafter and opened the gates of Paradise. Patrick's personal converts must have numbered into the hundreds of thousands before he made the sign of the Cross for the last time and laid him down to rest.

Patrick flashes the briefest of pictures for us of a baptismal ceremony of his time in Ireland in the *Letter:* the newly baptised were clad in white garments and anointed on their foreheads with chrism, the fragrant and consecrated oil.

This picture comes to us from the later period of Patrick's spiritual reign over Ireland, after he had been consecrated a bishop and the Roman Catholic Church was well established along the east coast of Ireland and the communicants confirmed in ritual. In the earlier days of his mission, baptism was probably more immediate and primitive, but no less effective. But, with his churches organised and backed financially by Rome, the converts were able to don the white garments symbolic of purity after the rites.

It was the day after such a mass ceremony that the raiders of Coroticus, slipping over conveniently from Dumbarton down the Firth of Clyde and across the narrow passage to that other coast where the grass seemed to grow greener, the cattle fatter and the women more delectable, found the newly baptised, the oil still glistening on their foreheads, and butchered them, keeping only the young and beautiful to be sold into slavery.

Patrick speaks also of booty taken which the jeering soldiers refused to return when he sent a native priest he had trained himself from childhood, accompanied by deacons and clerics, to demand the release of the baptised captives and the restoration of 'some of the booty,' a curious and intriguing phrase. Why only 'some' of the booty? Does it mean that Patrick was so thoroughly a man of his age as to recognise the rights of belligerents to their spoils as they existed in those days? Patrick, for instance, never protested against the institution of slavery itself, but only against the ill-treatment of slaves and particularly the debauchery of female slaves who were forced to brutal concubinage—a bondage, which, once he had baptised them, deeply concerned Patrick. He never asked the Irish to change their laws, but only their ways when their acts and behaviour conflicted with the Christian ethics.

What is probable is that now, in the later years, the greater part of Ireland was safely in the fold of the Catholic Church, with numbers of converts and churches far beyond what any of those doubting Thomases who originally opposed Patrick's mission might have imagined. It could well have been that the days of his primitive church and altar equipment, hand-forged and hand-sewn, were over and

that the larger of the Saint's establishments were by now
equipped with some of the more valuable treasures of the
mainland churches, loot to make the eyes of Coroticus's
apostate raiders sparkle.

The part of the spoils which Patrick may have asked to
have returned may have been those objects consecrated
to the Eucharist. The raiders, supposedly Romano-British
Christians but composed mainly, apparently, of Pictish-Irish
mercenary soldiery from the North of Britain—now Scotland—only laughed at the clerics, packed their booty and
captives into their ships and departed, having dealt a most
serious blow to Patrick's dignity and prestige.

In two paragraphs of the *Confessio* Patrick refers to the
manner of worship of the heathen Irish whom he came to
convert. He refers to their adoration of idols and things
impure. And close to the end he rises to his most graphic
and telling piece of writing: 'For this sun which we see rises
daily for us because He commands so, but it will never
reign, nor will its splendours last; what is more, those
wretched men who worship it will be miserably punished.
Not so we, who believe in, and worship the true sun, Christ.'

One's mind turns back to Patrick's account of his nightmare after the feast of roast pig during his journey with the
sailors, and his rescue from the black spell under which he
was enthralled by the rising of the sun, symbolic of the
relieving spirit of Christ. It could not have been too difficult
to transfer the worship of the pagans from the physical orb
of the sun, its delicious warmth and healing light, to that
same sun as a symbol of the warmth and light of Jesus.
Oft-times Patrick thundered, but there were times, too, when
he must have led the heathen-like children, left them their
customs and even some of their rites, but translated them
into Catholic worship.

The idols, however, he might well have overthrown, as is told in the legend of his destruction of the great gold- and silver-covered stone, Crom Cruaich, on the sanctuary of Mag Slecht, or the Plain of Slecht. When he had done so, a devil emerged from beneath it, whom Patrick fought and defeated, but in the fighting lost his favourite brooch and would not leave the scene until he had searched the grass and retrieved it. It was said further that many of the people of the plain never forgave Patrick for his destruction of their god and tried to kill him and that a number of the subsequent plots against his life stemmed from this deed.

There is no record of this event, nor does Patrick mention it anywhere in his brief written legacies. Nevertheless, in both *Confessio* and *Letter* there are echoes of that hatred that Patrick engendered in some of the Irish, and which hint of acts perpetrated against their faith more violent and injurious to the pride of a fierce, free people than the mere preaching of the Gospels. He 'suffers insults from the unbelievers, and many persecutions even unto bonds'; he is hated, despised by many, etc., etc.

The worship of idols has been anathema to the Church from its very inception and its loudest thunders have been loosed upon those who bowed down before them instead of lifting their faces to the God on high. The hatreds that seethed about Patrick in Ireland and often came close to costing him his life might have been like the distant flickering of lightnings reflecting something fearful, violent and magnificently courageous on Patrick's part that *did* take place by the sacred circuit of the twelve pillar stones of Mag Slecht.

A thousand miracles attributed to Patrick are narrated in the Lives. He himself tells of not a single one of these.

Yet he gives personal testimony to one miracle in which he participated, that of heavenly communication and prophecies borne out. And it is touching to find that even in that age, supposed to be more innocent and credulous, there were scoffers and unbelievers to whom Patrick had to address himself before announcing the wonders that had befallen him:

'And let those who will laugh and scorn—I shall not be silent; nor shall I hide the signs and wonders which the Lord has shown to me many years before they came to pass, as He knows everything even before the times of the world.'

The whole life of St Patrick—and this is the recurring theme that runs through his justification of himself to his enemies—was one long benign miracle in which the usual laws governing the success of man were truly set aside so that one selected by God might do His work, as He wished it done, in spite of the fury, self-satisfaction, arrogance and obstructionism of members of the human species.

CHAPTER FOUR

The Legendary Figure

I

PROBABLY never has a man been quite so falsified by legend, pseudo-history and propagandising hagiographers as St Patrick.

Never, too, it would seem, have the compilers of pious fiction paid less attention to making the character of their hero conform even in the slightest to that of the real man whose nature and personality revealed in the two documents in his own hand must have been ever before them.

For not only did they create, and cause to be handed on to succeeding ages and eras, a completely bogus Patrick, but they also set him in a bogus Ireland.

The Ireland of Tirechàn, Muirchu, and other early Christian writers and biographers was not the cheerful fairyland of leprechauns, 'little folk,' heroes and immortals and beauteous faerie queens, but instead a grim ante-room of Beelzebub peopled by savage and barbarous pagans thirsting for Christian blood, treacherous and murderous kings, daemons and evil Druid magicians, blasphemous thaumaturgs bent upon destroying Patrick. Miracles, good when performed by Patrick, bad when conjured by the mages, abounded. Humans could assume animal form. The weather was subject to the spells of wizards and Saint alike.

Through this gloomy setting moved Patrick, an irritable, vindictive old curmudgeon, preaching, converting, anathematising, withering, burning, slaying, sterilising, cursing the unborn child in its mother's womb, pronouncing maledictions upon families of generations to come, and comporting himself generally in a most un-Christian-like and ungentlemanly manner. His portraitists forgot or never appreciated that, whatever the shortcomings of his formal educations may have been, Patrick was born a Christian, a Roman citizen and a gentleman, and never at any time did he deviate from the character of any of these.

As an extreme example of one of the Patricks who 'lives' in the Ireland of today in the inherited memory of its natives, here is a pair of stories collected and set down from local people in the vicinity of Armagh in Ulster in the north of Ireland, the great bishopric supposed to have been founded originally by Saint Patrick. These stories were taken down verbatim by Dr T. F. G. Paterson, O.B.E., Curator of the County Museum at Armagh, by whose kind permission they are used:

THE STORIES MAY NOT BE TRUE

'The bull pushed over during the night all that Patrick set up be day. An' Patrick wus very annoyed an' cursed the bull an' it went mad. The whole of Armagh wus after it. It raged an' tore for miles around, but whether it wus killed be Patrick's curses, or died of a temper I don't remember.

'It was wonderful the way the saints cud curse in the oul' days. The same Patrick was good at it be all accounts. He'd ring he's bell on ye and curse ye for little. An' ride over ye if he tuk the notion. He killed he's sister that way [in punishment, legend-cum-gossip alleged, for having loved not wisely but too well]. An' ivery time she riz he turned the horses an' drew the chariot over her again. She soon died of it. But God wusn't always pleased with him for capers of that sort. He tried it once on a man but God raised the groun' an' the wheels did no damage.

That should have been a lesson to him. But the stories may not be true. The oul' people toul' them anyhow.'

AN' PATRICK LOST A TOOTH

'Shure Patrick was the one! He come here to Blackwater-town once an' he had a fight in the meadow with the oul' boy himself. An' the battle ended in the River Dabhall below ye. It's a pity indeed that the divil got away, but it's away he got. An' Patrick lost a tooth in the fight, on the brink of the water, an' it lay in it for many a year, until at last it was tuk intil the church.

'It wus here too the same Patrick met another saint whose name I clane forgit, but he didn't like him anyhow so he ordered he's coachman—for indeed the quality had such-like in them days too—to drive over the other fellow. But the driver wus afeared to run down a man that wus mebbe better than Patrick he's self. I have heard that the stories are in history so it's sacred truth they are.'

This particular tale—and the saint the narrator 'clane for-got' was St Olcan—occurs in the eleventh-century *Tripartite Life*, in which the story of the birth of this figure is a typical specimen of the literature of that era.

'Then Patrick went into Dal Araide and [afterwards] into Dal Riata. Then came Doro, king of Carn Sétnai in the north. He heard the crying of an infant out of the earth. The cairn is broken up, the grave opened. A smell of wine comes round them out of the grave. They see the live son with the dead mother, a woman who died of the ague. She was taken by them oversea to Ireland, and after her death brought forth the infant, who lived, they say, seven days in the cairn. "*Olc!* [bad] is that," saith the king. "Let Olcan be his name," saith the Druid. Patrick baptised him. He is Bishop Olcan of Patrick's household in Airthir Maige, a noble city of Dal Riatai.'

Eventually Bishop Olcan got into hot water with Patrick through becoming involved in a pretty little blackmail plot contrived by one Saran who had been excommunicated by Patrick. Saran took captives and threatened to kill them unless Olcan should give him heaven. Poor Olcan promised heaven to Saran and baptism.

'And they [Olcan] met at Cluain Fiacnae in the north on the road. "Drive the chariot over him," saith Patrick. . . . "I dare not," saith the charioteer, "make it go over a bishop." '

The rest of this passage is taken up with the curse that Patrick thereupon laid on Olcan. This was that Ireland and that Patrick.

Here is a typical folk tale of St Patrick from Connemara in County Mayo, condensed from the translation from the original Irish. The breadth of Ireland practically separates Connemara from Armagh, yet this tale has a great similarity to the story of King Daire and the bronze pot from overseas which begins this book. It is a representative early Christian morality tale and shows the Saint in softer and less vengeful mood.

A pagan chieftain by the name of Crom Dubh, who lived somewhere in Connaught near where Patrick was established engaged in bringing Christianity to the west, refused to be baptised but nevertheless was a friend of Patrick's—in fact, so good a one that when he slaughtered an ox he sent a quarter of the beast to Patrick by a servant as a gift.

When the servant returned, Crom Dubh queried the servant as to how Patrick had expressed his thanks for this princely present and was informed that the fellow had no idea. All Patrick had said was 'Deo Gratias' (Thanks be to God). Astonished, the chieftain sent Patrick another quarter to see whether this would elicit anything more fitting, and when the servant brought back nothing better than 'Deo Gratias' again, dispatched still a third quarter and for his pains got a third 'Deo Gratias.'

Enraged, Crom Dubh sent for Patrick. 'For,' tells the tale, 'it was Crom Dubh's intention to kill Patrick because the Saint did not give him great thanks and because he did not show his gratitude on bended knee for the three-quarters of an ox which he sent to him.'

When Patrick came, Crom Dubh reproached him first before proceeding with the killing saying that Patrick had failed to give great thanks for his gifts. Patrick argued that he had given great thanks and called for a scales. On one side of the scales a similar three-quarters of an ox was placed. Then Patrick wrote 'Deo Gratias' three times on a scrap of paper and placed it in the opposite balance pan. The paper weighed down the three-quarters of meat and was the heavier by far.

The 'he-got-the-job' or punch line is as modern as any moral or pious anecdote. 'Oh, Patrick!' cried Crom Dubh. 'It is I who have erred. For God's sake baptise me and my household and also those whom I rule. This day they must be converted to the Christian Faith.'

And so this is the reason why the last Sunday in July is called 'Crom Dubh's Sunday.' It is on this Sunday that the pilgrimage goes to Croagh Patrick in County Mayo.

There are curious overtones to this story as well as that of King Daire and the bronze pot. One is the light it throws upon the social usages amongst the kings of that age. Gifts called for effusive and at times close to servile (on bended knee) thanks, implying almost vassalage. And in all likelihood, from his six-year captivity in Ireland and his observance of customs, Patrick knew this very well and simply refused at any time to play *that* game. He bent the knee to none but

God. Such gifts as he accepted were in God's name and thanks were rendered to Him.

II

THE Irish from time immemorial have been fluent and imaginative cursers, the Druid getting his results by magic, the laymen by hopeful and wishful thinking. Hardly a king or hero chieftain or warrior but was labouring under some curse laid upon him, or striving to avert some dire prophecy. The Irish of old were quick-tempered, too; an insult did not have to be repeated twice: a curse, a blow, a flashing sword—the handshake and reconciliation would come afterwards . . . if there were survivors. This sensitivity, irritability and hair-trigger response, characteristics of an independent warrior people, were grafted on to Patrick by the hagiographers who were themselves Irish . . . and perhaps constitutionally irritable.

Patrick is charged with having cursed hills, lakes, rivers, the fish in them and the fishermen on them and trees and stones. Once in a particularly testy mood he is said to have caused a road to sink and swallow up a train of well-filled chariots which had refused to draw aside to allow him to pass—something every Sunday motorist has wished to be able to do at some time or other, but not exactly the attribute of a saint.

Another time Patrick cursed Ireland three times in his sleep. A servant who happened to be present and heard him quickly averted the curses to the tops of rushes, the lowing of kine and the ends of furze. The aversion of a curse to some other object, if one was in time, was a kind of insurance invented by the Irish, probably due to the prevalence of the curse as a weapon. At any rate, since that time the lowing of

Irish kine has had a peculiar note, and the tops of ferns and rushes have been withered brown.

But the greatest of all Patrick legends and stories of all the hundreds credited to him by his ancient biographers is that concerned with the great duel with Ireland at stake fought between Patrick and the High King of Ireland, Laoghaire (pronounced Leary) and his Druid mages, on the hill of Slane in Meath and in the great hall of the palace of the king at Tara.

The story is told by every biographer from Muirchu-maccu-Machtheni and Tirechàn on down. In its details it is questioned today from beginning to end, but there seems to have been truth in its essence. Patrick surely stood once upon the hill of Slane, looking across the lush valley to the distant ridge that was Tara where dwelt the man he must conquer. And as surely he once sat in the great banqueting hall of the High King at Tara, arguing, contending with and persuading him. Not all of the great Patrician Easter legend could have been invented.

The Hill of Slane has been occupied since the most ancient of times into the prehistoric. Muirchu refers to the place as the Graves of the Men of Fecc. It was an ancient burial ground, *Rath*, and later a Norman fortress. It lies in the valley of the Boyne, that most beautiful of all meandering, pastoral rivers, twelve miles from its mouth. It consists of a conical mound built up of layer upon layer of the history of Ireland, and bearing the ruins of an old stone church and college that once flourished on the site. There is a graveyard connected with the church ruins, but a more modern one. Beneath it no doubt rest the bones of the men of Fecc.

Tall oaks and copper beeches are reminders that the hill was once forested; cows ruminate on the pebbly slopes, and it is crowned by a huge fortress ring, mound and deep fosse, from which giant trees have sprouted. On a clear day you may look across the rich, green parklands of the Plain of Meath to the mound ten miles removed, that is Tara —that Tara through whose beamed halls that hallowed poet's harp once sounded; Tara the seat of the Irish High Kings; and now no more than a hill of archæological cairns, depressions, mounds and sites that mark where once stood the palaces and banqueting hall of the royal.

But, according to the story-tellers, high drama took place there one Easter, and it was on the Hill of Slane they had Patrick perform what, if even partly true, was the most courageous act of his Mission. For it was thither he repaired, unarmed and attended only by his clerics, to light the Paschal fire and challenge the authority of the High King Laoghaire.

The story is wonderfully woven and prepared for. King Laoghaire, his under-kings, nobles, Druids and bards were holding a great Council Feast in the long banqueting hall of Tara, the outlines of which may still be seen today in the form of depression on the hill-top. It was the custom that on the night of this great *Feis* or gathering, no fire was to be kindled until the King with appropriate ceremonies had lit the great fire heaped up in the royal enclosure. Thus the stage is set for Patrick to call attention to his mission and his God and throw down the gauntlet to the old order.

If you were on Tara in the dark of night looking out over the pitch black of the countryside you could not miss seeing the pinpoint of light from Patrick's blaze on Slane, shining across the plain of Breg. The High King saw and indignantly consulted his Druids, who said with that wonderfully pat prophecy which is the result of hindsight writing: 'O High King, unless this fire which you see be quenched this same night, it will never be quenched; and the kindler thereof will overcome us all and seduce all the folk of your realm.'

Alarmed, the King ordered nine chariots harnessed and with his Queen and magicians drove the ten miles from Tara to Slane, but paused outside the circle of Patrick's fire lest, as his magicians warned him, he be overcome by the stanger's magic. Instead Patrick was summoned to Laoghaire to account for his actions and during the disputation Lochru, one of the King's magicians blasphemed against the Christian Faith. Transfixing the blasphemer with a stern look, Patrick prayed to God that he be raised aloft and flung to the ground. Instantly Lochru was lifted into the sky by an unseen hand and then flung to earth so that his brains were dashed out upon a stone and he died.

The King commanded his men to kill Patrick, but the Saint cried: 'Let God arise and His enemies be scattered!'

'Then,' narrates Muirchu, 'straightway darkness came down, and a certain horrible commotion arose, and the ungodly men fought amongst themselves, one rising up against another, and there was a great earthquake. And He bound the axles of their chariots, and drove them with violence and they rushed in headlong flight, both chariots and horses, over the level ground of the great plain, till at last only a few of them escaped half-alive to the mountain of Monduirn; and at the curse of Patrick seven times seven men were laid low by this stroke in the presence of the King and his elders, until there remained only himself and his wife and two others of his companions; and they were sore afraid. So the Queen approached Patrick and said to him: "O man, righteous and mighty, do not destroy the King; for the King will come and kneel and worship thy Lord." And the King, compelled by fear, came and knelt before the Saint and feigned to worship Him whom he did not wish to worship.

'And when they had parted from one another, the King

went a little way, and called St Patrick by feigned words, minding to slay him by some means. But St Patrick, knowing the thoughts of the villainous King, blessed his companions [eight men and a lad] in the name of Jesus Christ and came to the King. The King counted them as they came; and straightway they were nowhere to be seen, taken away from the King's sight; but the heathen folk saw naught but eight stags and a fawn [the lad was Patrick's boy disciple, Benignus or Benen] going as it were to the wilderness. And King Loiguire, with the few that had escaped, returned at dawn to Temoria [Tara] sad, cowed and humiliated.'

This is rousing, lusty stuff, with the villains defeated with the aid of a bloodthirsty Old-Testament God. It had all the elements that went to make up a best-seller of the seventh or eighth century, and contained as much truth as the usual fictions of that type.

However, the tale is not yet done. The next day, Easter Sunday, his humiliation apparently forgotten after a good night's sleep, the King was feasting at Tara with his assembly when Patrick, attended by five companions, suddenly appeared at the banquet hall—having entered through closed doors as Jesus had once done—to take up the gage once more.

Only one man arose to honour him, Dubthach-maccu-Lugir, the chief poet of Ireland, who was an early convert. The High King hospitably invited Patrick to partake of food, and Lucetmael, the other chief Druid whose partner and companion Lochru had been killed the night before, demanded a further trial of powers.

Then began a duel of outdoor parlour magic on a grand scale between Lucetmael and Patrick, with Patrick giving as good as was sent and, as it developed, a little better. As an opener, the Druid wizard spiked Patrick's cup with a drop of poison. Patrick caught him at it, prayed and the liquor was turned into ice. When the Saint turned the cup upside down only the drop of poison fell out. Then he blessed the cup and the liquid was restored to its own nature to the marvel, and no doubt applause, of all.

Next, Lucetmael with incantations brought waist-high snow to the plain. Patrick said, in effect: Very good, but now let us see you get rid of it. The magician couldn't until the next day. The Saint pointed up the moral, saying: 'Thou art able to do evil, but not good; I am not of that sort.' Then he blessed the plain and the snow vanished.

The wizard muttered up a thick darkness. Patrick prayed it away and was acclaimed by all. The High King, however, wanted something conclusive and suggested that books of the two contending parties be thrown into the water and he would worship his which came unharmed. The Magus declined on the grounds that water was the Saint's God, having no doubt heard of the rite of baptism. The King next suggested that the sacred books be thrown into the fire. Lucetmael declined again on similar grounds, though here his Christian theology was less sound.

Patrick then suggested a test which seemed heavily loaded in favour of the wizard coming out of it with a whole skin. A house or hut was to be built in two sections, one of green, the other of dry wood. Lucetmael was to enter the green portion, clad in St Patrick's mantle. The Saint's young and ardent disciple Benen, wearing the Druid's cloak, would go into the dry portion. The house would then be set alight and the Most High would judge.

Lucetmael accepted and went to his predestined doom as he and the house of green twigs were utterly consumed, only the cloak of Patrick being spared by the fire, while Benen survived unharmed in his tinder box, only the cloak of the magician being burned to ashes.

King Laoghaire, according to the account of Muirchu Tirechàn and others, was not what might be called a good sport and game loser. Narrates Muirchu: 'And the King was greatly enraged against Patrick, because of the death of his magician, and he almost rushed upon him minding to slay him; but God hindered him. For at the prayer of Patrick and at his cry, the wrath of God fell upon the ungodly people and many of them perished.' Out of fear Laoghaire permits himself to be converted. However, this bit of the legend is directly controverted by the facts of early Irish history, which records Laoghaire as buried in pagan fashion, standing upright, his weapons to hand facing his old enemies, the men of Leinster, who had killed him. Or he died, during a campaign, of a lightning stroke.

III

In this grim counter-Druid and God-magician who plays with loaded dice and deals out death and destruction left and right, loosing a killing God indiscriminately, there is not the faintest resemblance to the honest, fair-minded, unvengeful Patrick of the *Confessio*, or to the God he loves so deeply and faithfully. The picture is wholly false and completely out of character. It is the beginning of the Druidising of the Saint. For in this battle, though he speaks with the words of God, and supposedly for Him, his deeds and behaviour are those of the pagan magicians against whom he was striving.

There is no doubt that in his time Patrick believed devoutly in the efficacy of prayer against the works of the devil and the machinations of demons, and he believed in the devils and the demons as well and their power to work evil amongst men. But this struggle was carried on not in the physical but in the spiritual plane.

Yet something tremendous did take place there in Meath, whether at Tara, or Slane, or both—something far more marvellous and astounding and to the credit of Patrick than any of the foregoing. From what evidence there is, plus tradition that lingers and will be heard, points to the fact that against the bitter opposition of the Druids Patrick talked King Laoghaire either into permitting him to preach and convert in the territory controlled by the High King, or to accept the fact of the establishment of a Christian Church in the north-eastern part of Ireland with Patrick as its head, and to call a conclave or assembly of kings, nobles and chief men of the island to resolve the position of this new group under Irish law. For if Laoghaire was the instigator of the *Senchus Mór*, as the first written legal code compiled during his reign was called, Patrick himself was a church lawyer with a keen sense of code and responsibility and the delegation as well as the fountainhead of authority. The two men had much in common.

Here is something which from the records points to an accomplished fact. Here for the first time, outside of the personal account that the Saint left behind him, one seems to encounter the solid, substantial bulk of Patrick.

Scholars turning to the ancient law tracts have unearthed texts indicating the extent of the christianising of the Tuaths by the end of Patrick's ministry. The Tuath was the basic independent state and political community in ancient Ireland, a group of free citizens not necessarily kin, consisting of nobles who were landowners, clients who rented or 'hired' land and so had a close bond with the owners of the property, skilled craftsmen and professional men, that is, lawyers, poets, teachers and Druids, etc.

The head of the Tuath was the king or chieftain. In size, a Tuath might be about a third the area of a modern Irish county. In some cases it might be contained in six hundred square miles. There were no cities in the Tuaths, but they were in a sense agricultural suburban communities with no *urbs*, the inhabitants living as neighbours adjoining one another's property but with no centre except the *Dun* or *Rath* of the king, which was visited by them only for purposes of political assembly.

That the size and organisation of the Tuath were practical for Patrick is indicated by the text, the *Riagail Padruic:* 'Here is what the testament of Patrick contains for the souls of the men of Ireland: Every Tuath should have a chief Bishop [*Prim-escop*], to ordain its clergy, to consecrate its churches, to give direction to its chiefs and nobles, and to sanctify and bless their children after baptism. For the Tuath and territory which have no bishops to discharge these functions see the law of their faith and belief perish.'

This text may well have been composed some time after Patrick's death, but it is in complete harmony with what is to be found in both the *Letter* and the *Confessio:* including the echo of the alarm expressed by Patrick in the latter document that, if he were to desert his post and return to his friends and kinsfolk in Britain and Gaul, the newly-made Irish Christians would tend to backslide and his work would be undone.

The legend connected with the composing of the *Senchus Mór*, the first written legal code of Ireland, compiled during the reign of the High King Laoghaire in the fifth century, as told in the introduction to this code, is that at Patrick's request a convention of all Ireland was held under the High King in order to bring the laws of Ireland into conformity with the ethics and spirit of the growing Christian communities.

How much truth is contained in the legend cannot be

D

ascertained, but the hand of Patrick—the acceptance of the
Christianisation of the Tuaths—must be seen in several of
the texts of the *Senchus Mór* which admit the bishop to equal
dignity with the king, the chief poet and the head of the
written law, emphasising their equal standing and importance
in various matters by refusing to allow any distraining against
them personally by reason of their elevation, rank and dignity.

Here we are conscious of a sharp dividing line between
the old and the new Ireland, the addition of a wholly new
institution and a new dignitary, the head of that institution,
to the national laws of Ireland, laws which, as we have seen,
in pre-Christian times governed and were extended into
every Tuath.

It is doubtful whether by his own nature, coupled with
the pressures of his advisers, King Laoghaire in opposition
to Christianity would have thought of this or granted
Christianity such recognition as to establish it almost as the
state religion, or, if not that, a religion at least protected by
the laws of the state. The impetus must have come from
Patrick.

Nor can those who argue the many Patricks fused into
one, or the non-existence of any one great missionary to
Ireland, very well deny that impetus to the author of the
Confession. Everything contained in that document points
to the author as the logical man to have brought about this
change; the number of his converts; the scope of his work;
the length of his residence in Ireland; and the power and
'exaltation,' to use his own word, of the position he achieved
there before his death.

Once the High King was in possession of the facts, and
his own sons and daughters were converted to this belief—
a belief which, incidentally, carried behind it the prestige of
the greatest power the world had ever known up to that

time, the Roman empire—once he knew of all the other princes, princesses and queens converted and the spread of the religion to the furthermost outposts of the realm, it would have been obvious to him that the battle was lost. One can then entertain the picture of two sensible and politically minded men sitting down together to discuss what had become a mutual problem, due to a *fait accompli*.

But it is quite possible that Patrick may originally have had to kindle that fire on the Hill of Slane to let the High King know that he was there and meant business.

How the Saint ever wrung permission from Laoghaire in the first place to proselytise in his territory remains one of the unsolved mysteries of the era and perhaps one of the true miracles of Patrick's apostleship and a great historic example of the power of faith to move mountains.

One partial solution, a hint of which is contained in the Easter legend of Slane and Tara outlined above, might rest in the power exercised by the women of Ireland and, in particular, by the queens, who by Irish law and custom were equal in dignity, property, worth and command to their husbands. Amongst the Picts, inheritance passed in the female line. In the great sagas of Ailill and Medb of Connacht, though Ailill is king, Medb is the predominant partner militarily as well as politically, taking the field to direct a war and accompanying the armies on the march.

A number of Irish kings, chieftains and princes were known to have had British wives, many of whom would have been Christians, or at least, through birth and education, highly susceptible to Christianity.

The legend connected with the foundation of the Christian community at Trim, the 'ford of the alder' on the River Boyne, west of Tara, has such a British queen at its centre.

Here, one Fedilmid, son of King Laoghaire had his *Dun*.

His wife was a British lady and either already a Christian, or thoroughly familiar with the faith. According to the tradition of the district, and as *The Tripartite Life* tells it:

'When Patrick came with his vessels to Ireland to preach to the Gael, and when he went to Tara, he left Lomman [one of Patrick's British bishops] in the estuary of the Boyne, keeping his ship for the forty nights of the Lent. Patrick ordered him to row his vessel against the Boyne till he should get to the place wherein Ath Truimm stands today. Ath Truimm was at that time the stronghold of Feidlimid son of Loegaire, son of Niall. In the morning, Fortchern son of Fedilmid went and found Lomman with his gospel before him. A marvel to him [Fortchern] was the doctrine he heard. He believed and was baptised by Lomman and Fortchern was listening to the doctrine until his mother came a-seeking him. She made welcome to the clerics for of the Britons was she, namely, Scoth, daughter of the King of Britons. Fedilmid himself came to have speech of Lomman, and he believed, and he offered Ath Truimm to God and to Patrick and to Lomman and to Fortchern.'

Whatever the truth of how this meeting came about, whether as fortuitous or accidental as the story pretends, or whether carefully arranged by Patrick who foreknew that he would find a friend at Ath Truimm, the fact remains that here was a British queen, a Christian who permitted her son to be baptised and strongly influenced her husband not only to accept the faith itself, but to donate land for the foundation of a church.

One could almost read the workings of the mind of a master tactician on the move. In the person of his son, his daughter-in-law and his grandson, Christianity had already come very close to the High King, and his own wife may have been a further influence upon him to permit Patrick to pursue his ways. The appeal of Christianity to women was strong, often stronger than its message to men. It struck hard in certain kinds of men, but seemed to have a direct appeal to all women.

Anyone who reads between the lines of the *Confessio* must become aware that Patrick himself had a powerful influence over women and that he attracted them. The person and personality of the evangelist have never been a negligible feature of conversions. If the eye of woman lingers upon him through whose being God's message is filtered, it is no more than human and natural, and likely enough the will of God whose instrument the apostle has become.

IV

ON page after page of legend, miracle story and manuscript buried in monastery libraries you will find that other Patrick —who never existed—wandering about Ireland bringing the promise of the gospels, but also working much mischief upon pagans who, if not wholly innocent, were to say the least bewildered by this short-tempered man who went cursing and punishing and death-dealing across the length and breadth of their land with a vindictiveness that is little short of startling. Nothing escaped his short temper and vengefulness. At Druimm Conchinn in Mairg, for instance, the cross-beam of Patrick's chariot broke as he was on his way to Munster. There were woods on the ridge where this occurred and a new piece was made. It broke at once. Another tree was selected. This likewise collapsed. Relates *The Tripartite Life:* 'Patrick declared that never would any building be made of the wood of that grove. Which thing is fulfilled. Even a skewer is not made of it. Patrick's hermitage stands there; but it is waste.'

Occasionally a spark of humour illuminates the grim procession of church foundings, curses, rewards, punishments, foiling of attempted ambushes and poison plots, biter-bit stories and the like. In Cashel hard by Tipperary— Cashel, that stark rock rising from the green plain, that once was Sid-Druim, a hill of the *Sidhi* or faerie-folk—Patrick preached to, converted and baptised Oengus, King of Munster. The ceremony took place atop the limestone rock by the Coronation Stone of the kings of Munster. Near its close Patrick noticed that in the vehemence of his exhortation the pointed end of his crozier had pierced the royal convert's foot and blood was streaming therefrom on to the ground.

'Said Patrick: "Why didst thou not tell this to me?" Oengus replied: "It seemed to me that it was a rite of the faith." '

The legends, it must be noted, were as quick to lead Patrick to rewards as to curse. 'Thou shalt have its reward,' saith Patrick. 'Thy successor shall not die from a wound from today for ever.'

Yet an odd germ of truth may lurk in this story, too human and amusing perhaps to be entirely invented. It appears to be in keeping with the intensity of Patrick's faith. Once he was launched into his discourse praising the Lord and quoting the Saints of the Gospels, he would be transported, for this was his whole life.

That other Patrick had his gentler moments, too, in the inventive minds of his biographers, as when ashore between St Patrick's Isle in the Skerries and Drogheda in Sescnen's Valley they tell of how he was weary and lay down on the grass to sleep. A child, young Benen, son of Sescnen, feeling a surge of love for this stranger, gathered a bunch of meadow flowers and laid them on the breast of the Saint. Patrick awoke to hear the boy being reproved by his elders, and said: 'Trouble him not. He will be the heir of my kingdom.' This is one of the stories that ties Patrick in with the foundation of Armagh, the purpose behind at least one of the early biographies. The person and character of Benignus is re-encountered throughout the Patrick saga. He is the boy who enters the hut of dry wood during Patrick's duel with the Magi of Tara's High King; he is that same boy who is turned into a fawn as Patrick and his companions are taken for deer by the King-in-ambush.

Again a gentle side of Patrick is shown in the tale of an instance where he preached for three days and three nights and Saint Brigid, then a little girl, fell asleep and Patrick signalled that she was not to be disturbed. Later when she awakened he is said to have inquired politely of her as to the nature of her dreams.

A grateful Patrick—in a setting which gives an inkling, perhaps, of the command of his presence and the sincerity and clarity of his visage—is portrayed in the story of Dichu's Barn in Saul, which is located in that exquisite rolling country in the vicinity of Downpatrick and the landlocked salt sea Lough of Strangford. In Patrick's time this was a part of ancient Ulidia and within reach of Mount Slemish, the place of his captivity.

This is glacial country of low hills and ridges and wonderfully fertile valleys through which meander streams, burns and little rivers that empty into the Loch. From the highest of these hills over the sweet green pasture land the blue of the Loch and the silver of the sea may be viewed while to the south lie the sombre shapes of the melodically named Mountains of Mourne.

This section, now a region of scattered farms, was in Patrick's time thickly populated and wealthy. There are vestiges of Raths on almost every rise surrounding Saul:

Strangford at the mouth of the Lough was the seaport base of an enormous trade; the Mountains of Mourne constituted the landfall for the seaborne traders returning from export-import trips to Gaul and Bristol at the end of the Severn Estuary. This was the one spot in Ireland in almost constant touch with the mainland and the neighbour island of Great Britain. Here, if anywhere, would have been colonies of Christians, and most certainly the inhabitants of this teeming, busy area were familiar with Christianity.

Atop one of these rounded hills lived a chieftain by the name of Dichu. Dichu, at least, is a real character, historically attested in the *Annals of Ireland* he had two brothers who occupied Raths near by; he was accounted a good man.

The sea has slipped away from what then purported to be the landing place of Patrick at the mouth of the Slan River— now a small burn that flows beneath the road leading from Saul to Strangford—and green meadows feed cattle where once the tides lapped.

Dichu's swineherd, guarding his pigs on the slopes of Saul, saw the landing of the strangely clad men, men garbed and tonsured as he had never seen before. He took them for raiders of some new kind and ran to report the danger to his master.

Dichu whistled up his savage wolfhound, picked up spear, sword and shield and went forth to meet the danger head-on. Patrick advanced alone and the two men encountered one another in a field on one of the gentle hillsides.

By chanting the prophetic verse from the psalm '*Ne tradas, Domine, bestiis animas confitentes tibi,*' Patrick quelled the wolfhound, according to the story. Then something happened which in truth often does in life. Two strangers, one hostile and suspicious, faced one another, and suddenly knew that they liked one another and would be friends.

Dichu looked into the face of Patrick and was calmed as was his dog. Good called to good; brave and honest heart responded to a kind and decent man. Muirchu and *The Tripartite Life* each tell of this in the line from *The Life*, '. . . when he [Dichu] beheld the countenance of St Patrick, the Lord turned his thoughts to good,' of the former, and '. . . when Dichu saw Patrick, grief of heart seized him, and he believed and Patrick baptised him.'

Dichu then presented to Patrick a barn which stood on a rise not far from the home of the chieftain. This barn the Saint consecrated as his first church in Ireland. This district remained Patrick's favourite, and it was to the Church of the Barn of Duchu that legend has Patrick returning at the end of his life to die. In gratitude for Dichu's friendship and his gift, Patrick spoke a kind of poem to him, so wrote the old monks in their monastery cells, and the poem went something like this:

> 'God's blessing on Dichu
> Who gave me the Barn!
> May he have afterwards,
> A heavenly home, bright, pure, great!
> God's blessing on Dichu,
> Dichu and all his children,
> No child, grandchild or descendant of his
> Shall die but after a long life.'

Time has left little of the site of Dichu's Barn where legend for once shows Patrick's heart throbbing with joy. A Protestant church has been built there. Close by there still stands a piece of the wall of the old Church, the Catholic one that must have been erected there upon the site of Patrick's dearly beloved Barn until Cromwell's men toppled it. Dressed stones from this ancient church are to be seen in the walls that divide the fields, and littering the ground where they were tumbled centuries ago in that mysterious by-product of man's love for God—man's inhumanity to man.

Whether these tales be legend or truth, the district beyond the borders of Catholic Ireland, in Protestant Ulster, seems to vibrate with the presence of Patrick.

Not far off is Downpatrick, built upon the site of the ancient fortress of Dun-da-leth-glaisse, and here in the churchyard of St Patrick's Cathedral, in the midst of the thrice ringed and moated fortress, is the most astonishing falsification of all—a stone engraved with the ancient Celtic Cross and part of the name of PATRICK, purporting to cover the grave of St Patrick. But the stone is modern—of the last hundred years—and no one today knows where St Patrick is buried, or whether his venerated bones still lie undisturbed.

Local legend is strong that he once was interred there, and that at one time his remains were combined with those of Saints Brigid and Columbcill, and there is a piece of local doggerel that goes:

'In the grave three saints do fill,
Patrick, Brigid and Columbcill.'

The Saints are supposed to have rested in that vicinity, beneath the altar of the Catholic Church that once stood upon the site now occupied by the Protestant Cathedral, but where that altar stood has been forgotten, and the remains of all three were supposed to have been routed out and scattered by the men of Henry the Eighth and lost for ever to the devotions of the faithful.

V

THE curiously irritable nature that St Patrick acquired in Irish folk-lore is an interesting sidelight upon the fact that his biographers were not writers, but monks. When they found it necessary to invent, they did so without thought as to the reflection upon the character of the principal in the story as a writer would have done.

The tale of the bishopric of Strongman Macc Cairthinn is a case in point. 'Once as Patrick was coming from Clochar from the north, his champion, to wit, Bishop Macc Cairthinn, lifted him over a difficult place. This is what he said after lifting Patrick: "Oh, oh!"

' "My God's doom!" saith Patrick, "it was not usual for thee to utter that word."

' "I am [now] an old man and I am infirm," saith Bishop Macc Cairthinn, "and thou hast left my comrades in churches and I am still on the road."

' "I will leave thee then in a church," saith Patrick, "that shall not be very near lest there be familiarity, and shall not be very far so that mutual visiting between us be continued." '

The story accounts for the establishment of the bishopric of Clogher, presenting a sweet picture of a great giant grown old and infirm in loyal service receiving his reward, but the other side of the medal is a cold Patrick who has taken the lifetime service of this man for granted and never noticed that he was ageing, weakening and no longer capable of carrying out his arduous duties, having to be reminded that his most faithful of servants has been overlooked. Nor does Patrick's response to his strongman's plea appear to be kindly, but on the other hand even grudging. The hand that wrote this dipped its pen neither into the ink of truth nor of love.

It would be fascinating to know whence Patrick's bio-graphers writing anywhere from two to five centuries after his death derived their familiarity with the oaths of the Saint which add to the picture of the testy and easily irritated old man.

'My God's doom,' appears again and again in *The Tripartite Life*, a phrase which would seem to verge close upon blas-phemy. There is no such saying in the *Letter to the Soldiers of Coroticus*, in which the Saint is really filled with righteous anger; in fact there is no curse at all in this document. The strongest expletive that Patrick permits himself in the *Confessio* is: 'I know not, God knoweth.'

Muirchu, who wrote closest to Patrick's time, seems to be the authority for Patrick's favourite curse of '*Mudebrod*,' or '*Mudebroth*.'

'The learned tell of a man who lived in the Plain of Inis who was exceedingly harsh, and so grasping, and had run into such a pitch of folly and avarice that one day when the booby saw the two oxen that drew St Patrick's wagon rest-ing and grazing, after their holy labours, in a meadow of his farm, the silly man violently and inconsiderately drove them off by force in the very presence of Patrick.

'And St Patrick, enraged with him, said: "*Mudebrod!* thou hast done ill; this field of thine shall be of no profit to thee or to thy seed for ever; it shall be useless from this moment." And so it came to pass; for an overflowing inundation of the sea came on that very day and flowed around and covered the whole field; and as the prophet says: "A fruitful land was turned into a salt marsh for the wickedness of them that dwelt therein." It is therefore sandy and barren from the day on which St Patrick cursed it to the present time.'

The philologists have guessed at the origins of *Mudebroth* as stemming either from the British '*Muin Duiu Braut*' (My

God will judge) or the Irish '*Atbiur mo debroth*' (Pledge my
God's Doom) and by usage to have been pulled together
into the colloquialism *Mudebroth*, as in the tale of Daire,
'*Gratias Agamus*' (Let us give thanks) became *Gratzacham*.

Could Muirchu have heard it from one whose father's
great-grandfather remembered his own grandfather telling
of the day he was present when Patrick preached from a hill,
or baptised by a burn or well, and gave vent to the expletive?

Tradition is sometimes more to be trusted than written
records, particularly in a country such as Ireland where in
the early days there was no written record and history was
handed down by the poets in the form of sagas and memory
was cultivated far beyond what it is today. In pre-Christian
Ireland every educated man's head was the storehouse for
the archives of the nation.

The astonishing thing is that in the case of Patrick tradition and hand-me-down memory have shot so wide of the
mark in presenting a true, or even close-to-truth, portrait of
a man supposedly so greatly beloved. At times it would
seem that the distortion was almost deliberate, a curious
kind of vengeance upon the man who turned them from
the less taxing ways of their fathers into the rocky path of
truth from which thereafter there was not to be any
escape.

The distortion must have begun soon after his death and
continued down to modern times, wherein took place one
of the most startling perversions of all—the attempt to make
a Protestant Saint out of this very orthodox Catholic man
who was born, raised, lived and died an ardent Roman
Catholic in an age almost a thousand years before the first
voices of Protestantism were raised.

The death legend of the Saint shows him as wishing to
repair to Armagh to die and even setting out upon the

journey thither, when he is halted by an angel sent by his
own patron Angel Victor, a character taken from Patrick's
own account of the messages he received from the mysterious
Victoricus in his dreams, and who runs through all of the
biographies and Lives.

The angel said to him: 'Wherefore dost thou set out without the advice of Victor?' When Patrick asked what it was
he ought to do, he was commanded to return to Saul. He
did so, and in that sweet and gentle country was given the
last rites by Bishop Tassach—who through the long years
of his church foundations had been his artificer—and there
died.

Night refused to fall for twelve days after Patrick's death
and there were other miraculous manifestations of man's,
God's and nature's grief over the passing of this holy person.
By direction of an angel, his burial place was left to the
chance direction of two oxen turned loose to wander with
his body where they would. They lay down at Dun-da-
leth-glaisse and there Patrick was interred.

A near war blew up between the men of Ui-Neill and the
men of Airthir on one side, and the men of Ulaid on the other,
over possession of the body. The two parties who had been
neighbours and kinsmen rushed to arms, but a sudden rising
of Strangford Lough prevented the battle, and a miraculous
illusion, whereby the body thought to be in possession of the
men of Ui-Neill, oxen, wagon and all, suddenly vanished,
prevented a second clash, and eventually there was peace
between the two factions.

All of the stories have the appearance of face-savers. The
insistence of the Armagh propagandists that Patrick when
he felt his dissolution imminent wished to die in that See
and commenced a journey thither seems to point up the
fact that Patrick actually did retire to the peace and quiet

of Saul and the Church of Dichu's Barn in his last years and
that he actually did die there, which event had somehow
to be excused and explained. The second legend similarly
indicates that his wish was to be buried there as well. There
was nothing to cause Patrick to wish to lie at Dun-da-leth-
glaisse, now Downpatrick. The richest of his memories were
connected with Saul.

In *The Tripartite Life*, whose anecdotes, like false pearls
strung together on a thread, have contributed so greatly to
the distorted picture of Ireland's patron Saint—and which are
attributed to Columb-Cille, Bishop Ultan, Bishop Adamnan
Eleran, Ciaran, Bishop Ermedach of Clochar, Colman and
Presbyter Collait of Druim Roilgech, sources all lost, but
apparently examined by Muirchu, Tirechàn and others—
the compilation ends with the following valedictory:

'A righteous Man verily was this man, with purity of
nature like the patriarchs. A true pilgrim like Abraham.
Mild, forgiving from the heart like Moses. A praiseworthy
psalmist like David. A student of wisdom like Solomon. A
choice vessel for proclaiming righteousness like Paul the
apostle. A man full of the grace and the favour of the Holy
Spirit like John the child. A fair herb-garden with plants of
virtues. A vine-branch of fruitfulness. A flashing fire with
the fervour of the warming and heating of the sons of Life,
for kindling and for inflaming charity. A lion through
strength and might. A dove for gentleness and simplicity.
A serpent for prudence and cunning as to good. Gentle,
humble, merciful unto the sons of Life. Gloomy, ungentle
to the Sons of Death. A laborious and serviceable slave to
Christ. A king for dignity and power as to binding and
loosing, as to liberating and enslaving, as to killing and
giving life.'

All biographers, chroniclers, analysts, etc., accept the date of St Patrick's death as March 17th, but the year, and his age, already in dispute in the seventh century, remain unsolved to this day.

For what manner of man Patrick really was, we must turn once more to the testimony of his own hand.

CHAPTER FIVE

Patrick the Man

I

WHAT was St Patrick really like? What manner of man was he? What was his personal appearance? What kind of picture may we form of this mysterious, shadowy figure whose accomplishments were so fabulous, staunch, long-lived and concrete, but whose personality remains so elusive and nebulous?

Most of the answers lie in the, in itself, somewhat shadowy realm of deductive conjecture.

If ever there was delineation of the features of St Patrick on parchment, carved out of wood, or chiselled in stone, none has survived. In one of the chapels of the Cathedral at Armagh there is a battered piece of sculpture, a badly damaged and grotesque head which, it has been suggested, may represent or attempt to represent Patrick. The face is of repelling ugliness. There is no more reason why it should have been an attempted portrait of the Saint than any of the heads half effaced by time which adorn the ruins of ancient churches here and there. Besides which, churches in Patrick's time were built of wood, or clay and wattles, and there is no evidence of any contemporary Irish sculpture, in stone or any other portraiture material. The graphic arts do not appear to have flourished in ancient Ireland.

The modern, and of course completely anachronistic presentation in the unimaginative statuary of the Saint that one comes across here and there in Ireland—notably at the beginning of the pilgrimage climb to the summit of Croagh Patrick in the west—is that of a stalwart man in bishop's mitre and vestments grasping a long crozier and concealing his face behind a flowing white beard. The figure is as cold and empty as the stone from which it is carved. Not once has any modern native artist attempted to create a figure that would symbolise the God-given dynamic force of the man, or the lightnings of the spirit that flashed forth from the rough-garbed monk who was Patrick.

Nor have any of his many biographers attempted to present a physical picture of the man about whom they were writing, with the single exception of Jocelyn, who, writing a Life of St Patrick in the twelfth century, speaks of Patrick as being of low stature.

Was this a guess on Jocelyn's part? Or a deduction from the fact that the Saint as a grown man had Strongman Macc Cairthinn to carry him dry-shod through river fords? Or did this monk delve more deeply into the two documents written by Patrick himself, the Letter and the Confessio, and from the character revealed there read a person of slight rather than great physical stature?

For the psyche of the self-deprecating, sensitive and sometimes suspicious man that emerges from these documents is not one which would seem to fit into the frame of a big, burly, self-confident person. This is not to say that a big man cannot suffer from a feeling of inferiority as well as the little fellow, but he more often does not. True, the small man usually compensates for his lack of size by pushing and thrusting his way about with extra aggressiveness, which is not the case with Patrick. If anything, the Saint suffers from an over-supply of modesty, some of which does not ring quite true, with considerable pride of accomplishment breaking through the protestations of wretchedness and nothingness. But he doesn't *feel* like a tall man of imperious and commanding presence.

Yet neither does he sound like one of those really little men, snapping and yapping and trying to outbustle the world. He must fall somewhere between, a man of medium but not imposing height, tough, wiry, well-knit and well-muscled as only a man could be who had come through six years of slavery outdoors in every kind of weather, whose activities included riding over miles of tracks and bumpy roads in springless chariots, marching long distances, assisting in the building operations of his churches, and who, outside of one nose-bleed and an occasional lost tooth, never reported a day sick.

The colour of his eyes and hair and the shape of his features could be nothing but sheer guesswork, but one thing is certain, he was not ill-favoured. He was highly attractive both to men and to women and, if you will remember, to the child Benen.

The qualities in a man which are universally attractive to both men and women are strength, character, nobility and command rather than beauty. Women do not like pretty men, nor do men. There is no such thing as an ugly man if the eyes are filled with gentleness and intelligence and the spirit of goodness shines from within. Cruelty, megalomania, avarice, viciousness and an evil nature leave their marks upon a countenance. Equally, a great soul cannot conceal itself. The mark of dedication lies upon the brows of great men. When Patrick talked about his love for Christ and God, he must have been as beautiful and compelling as any man who ever walked the face of the earth.

Indications are that he was not bearded. The Roman clergy of his day were smooth-shaven. His tonsure was the Roman *corona*, a manner of cutting the hair of the clergy in imitation of Christ's crown of thorns which is still practised today in certain monastic orders. The head is shaved bald in the centre, leaving a ring of hair. The long robes and bishop's vestments in which he is usually depicted were ceremonial garbs donned for the celebration of the Eucharist, or when he went to confer with some king upon equal footing, and countered the rich garb of the nobility—the beautifully dyed linens, cloaks of wool and outer garments decorated with gold necklaces, bracelets, pins and brooches—with the equally impressive vestments of the church.

But they were hardly practical for trekking over wild country, rough moorland terrain and muddy tracks in the *fochla* or 'Chief's seat' of a two-wheeled chariot in all kinds of Irish weather, even though the vehicle was equipped with awning or hood overhead. Patrick's garb was probably a combination of the Irish and Continental monastic. He would have found the tight Irish trousers or *trews*, which descended from hips to ankle, useful in the field, even though later there appeared a canon in the Irish church forbidding the clergy to wear those close-fitting trousers. A simple shirt or tunic would have encased the upper part of his body, either of bleached linen, or saffron dyed which was the Irish custom, and over all the monk's robe with cowl of undyed wool, in grey, or bleached white.

His hands would have been rough and calloused, for they were no strangers to the tools of digging and building, particularly if Patrick was a monastery-trained missionary, which seems evident from his immediate establishment of the monastic system in Ireland. The Gallic missionary trainees of that era, as today, were taught to peel off and pitch in. One may well allow that when land had been given and there was a foundation to be dug and a church to be reared, the cleric's habit was not long slipping from Patrick's shoulders, leaving the man of action clad in breeks and tunic, wielding pick and mattock, particularly in the early days of his mission before so much of his time was taken up with details of organisation.

His disciples or students, those young native boys whom he was training into an Irish clergy, must have toiled at his side, and it is not difficult to form a picture of Patrick pausing for a moment in work to wipe the sweat out of his eyes and improve the moment of rest by catechising his pupils, or going over some point of ritual to be learned. Patrick accomplished so much in the brief span allotted him that it could only have been done by using every available moment.

The Saint had a succession of chariot drivers during his residence in Ireland, but there is indication that he could handle the reins himself and occasionally did.

Patrick had an unlimited supply of energy and drive which exhausted and left behind his less zealous and selfless companions. But he drove no one harder than he drove himself. He appears to have had a body of iron. Towards the end of his life it must have exhibited a mass of scars from chariot spills and accidents which were unavoidable, ambuscades and plots against his life, captures and beatings and the chafings and gyves and irons with which he was bound, types of which may be seen today in the National Museum in Dublin. The wear and tear upon the frame of Patrick during his twenty to thirty years of proselytising the Irish must have been such as to send an ordinary man into an early grave. Only a physically powerful and fit human being could have survived such hardships. He seemed to be immune to pain, imperturbable in the face of threats, and a stranger to ease or comfort.

Coupled with this physical stamina was an overwhelming moral and spiritual force and the record of it is to be read in the two documents that Patrick left behind him and the one possible contemporary estimate of him thought to have survived, the Hymn of Saint Secundinus on St Patrick.

How is it that one can come to love a man from something he wrote and was fifteen hundred years ago? This is one of the great and continuing graces of literature and that power of the human sometimes to put himself on paper in a guise as vital and lasting as ever he was—more so, in fact, in this case: for Patrick is mingled with the dust of Ireland of fifteen centuries, but his words still trumpet through the halls of time; and his personality, his character and nature, his strength and his weakness, his fears and his doubts, but, above all, his inextinguishable faith, emerge unchanged from the pages as though he had written them today and we had known him as friend, neighbour and fellow human being.

II

WHILE there is no doubt as to the authorship of the *Letter* and the *Confessio* or to the century when it was written, scholars are not so certain of the period of the adulatory hymn written by Bishop Secundinus, or Sechnall, as he was known in Ireland. As with everything having to do with Patrick, it is bound up with a legend that Secundinus, who supposedly—though without any existing recorded confirmation—was a nephew of Patrick, criticised his uncle for failing to preach charity, the charity, that is, of the layman who gives to the church and to the clergy.

Patrick, who had not an ounce of covetousness in him, or, if he had, had brought it well under control, replied with some asperity—for he did not take kindly to criticism—that it was for charity's sake that he did not preach charity, for, were he to do so, such a flood of gifts would result that not so much as the yoke of two chariot-horses would be left for any of the other saintly toilers on the island, present or future.

Secundinus, then, is supposed to have composed his hymn to mollify his uncle. It is filled with extravagant adulation and pious phraseology, yet here and there occur lines that furnish us with the only possible glimpse of Patrick as another living man saw him—if indeed this piece of writing is contemporary, as Prof. Bieler believes, and was written some time between the *Letter* and the *Confessio*, possibly in a defence of Patrick made necessary by the criticism and uproar against the Saint brought on by his firm and uncompromising stand against Coroticus.

Secundinus uses the word that so many others have had to apply to Patrick, 'steadfast in his faith'—again, the steadfast man. 'The gates of Hell will not prevail against him.' The comparison with Peter was apt, for the Irish church was founded upon the rock of Patrick.

Bishop Secundinus was the first to make use of that somewhat irritating and disagreeable booster's concept, the salesman of God that has come to haunt the modern evangelist, when he wrote:

'He sells the choice talents of Christ's Gospel
 And collects them among the Irish heathen with usury.'

He presents a picture of a man not content with the service of words alone but who knew the value of example:

'He gives the good an apostolic example and model
 . . . he inspires with good conduct.'

Patrick is not a prideful man, Secundinus tells us: 'Humble is he of mind and body because of his fear of God.' He might have added that Patrick was by nature an humble man, yet, as we shall see, he had his moments of towering pride and dignity, the dignity of a servant of God that is not to be brought low in the eyes of man.

The poet marks one physical aspect of Patrick: 'In his holy body he bears the marks of Christ.' The implication is that at some time during his life the stigmata were to be found upon the person of Patrick as they appeared centuries later upon the body of Saint Francis of Assisi. Yet there is another interpretation that may be placed upon this line, namely that the sufferings that Patrick had endured for Christ during the course of his apostleship to the Irish—tortures yet short of the martyrdom he would gladly have endured,—beatings and even sword-cuts and spear-thrusts had left their marks, as surely as a soldier grown old in service is able to trace the campaigns in which he fought by the cicatrices they have left upon his person.

Patrick was chaste. He tells us so himself, though he may not always have been so, and he indicates that he was not immune to the temptations and torments of the flesh. But from the time he came to Ireland, if not from the time he began to study for ordination to prepare himself to answer the call of the Irish, Patrick practised what he preached, and Secundinus corroborates it in the following stanza:

'He preserves his body chaste for love of the Lord,
    This body he has made a temple for the Holy Spirit,
And he keeps it such by purity in all his actions,
    He offers it as a living sacrifice acceptable to the Lord.'

There is in Secundinus yet another corroboration of a statement in one of Patrick's texts, and a most curious one. It will be remembered that nowhere is there any written record of Patrick's consecration as a bishop, by whom, or where; Patrick himself is silent upon the subject, and unless somewhere sometime a contemporary document is unearthed with some reference to this important event, or it is found to be mentioned in some yet undiscovered but reliable source, it must remain one of the many unsolved mysteries connected with the life of the Saint.

Patrick's sole reference to his high office is contained in the opening lines of the *Letter:* 'I, Patrick, a sinner, unlearned, resident in Ireland, declare myself to be a bishop. Most assuredly I believe that what I am I have received from God.'

Secundinus corroborates it in this fashion: 'For his merits the Saviour has raised him to the dignity of a bishop.'

How, besides, does this Frenchman (Secundinus came from Gaul) see his chief and co-worker? He writes that Patrick despised all worldly glory, that adversity pleased him, since it put him on his mettle and that, in the manner of many dedicated men, prophets, priests, scientists, scholars, poets, his eye is not upon the immediate, but from the distance of worldly detachment contemplates the rolling breakers of the eternal years. 'He is not,' writes Secundinus, 'moved by the violence of this world.'

Further, in this poem you will find proof of Patrick's orthodoxy: *what* it was he believed, preached and taught:

'Hymns and the Apocalypse and the Psalms of God
   he sings,
And explains them for the edification of God's people.
What he tells them he believes in the Trinity of the
   Holy Name
And teaches them that there is only one substance in
   Three Persons.'

The Father, the Son and the Holy Ghost; the Holy Spirit poured forth abundantly. This was Patrick's creed, and it appears likewise in his statement of it early in the *Confession*, which ends with: 'And Him do we confess and adore, one God in the Trinity of the Holy Name.'

There is further corroboration of Patrick's orthodoxy by this European bishop when he describes the Saint as: 'A faithful witness of the Lord to the Catholic Law.' The line speaks volumes, for it was written in an era when the church was yet young and not yet as strongly organised as it would be later. Deviations and heresies were rife; the minds and hearts of men the Christian world over had not yet been wholly absorbed or disciplined. A Pelagius with his denial of the doctrine of original sin could threaten to shake the very foundations of the Church and send prelates hurrying to all the corners of the Christian lands to combat it.

But of the Catholicity and discipline of Patrick there was no doubt, and his fellow worker confirms it. Isolation in Ireland had not changed Patrick. It never did. It was Patrick who changed Ireland.

One final glimpse of Patrick at work and of that work is granted us by Secundinus and, oddly, this time cross-corroborated by Patrick, with the *Letter* providing yet another link between the two men.

Bishop Secundinus tells: 'He frees captives from a two-fold servitude; the great numbers whom he liberates from bondage to men, these countless ones he frees from the yoke of the devil.'

If we turn now to *The Letter*, we find: 'This is the custom of the Roman Christians of Gaul: they send holy and able men to the Franks and other heathen with so many *solidi* to ransom baptised captives,' and the statement of Secundinus becomes clear.

In Patrick's time, the fifth century, Christian communities concerned themselves with the buying of Christian slaves—

the baptised ones, that is—out of captivity and providing the
purchase price necessary to buy their freedom. There would
be, it would seem, another powerful motive behind this
other than ordinary Christian charity, for this charity did
not extend to the non-Christian slave, and it was not the
institution of slavery itself that the Church condemned.

But the custom of ransoming Christian captives in those
days must in itself have provided a strong impetus for the
pagan to accept the new faith, to 'join the club,' as it were,
for it provided him with a kind of security he had never had
before. In addition to the promise of the 'life everlasting,'
there was the practical 'captivity insurance,' which assured
him that should he ever fall victim to a pirate or slave raid,
or be captured as a prisoner-of-war, as a baptised Christian
he would not vanish for ever into the limbo of the enslaved,
but those back home would not only concern themselves
about his fate, but would do something concrete about it.

Just as money is collected today for missionary work, for
the Red Cross, abused Hungarians, or victims of flood or
earthquake, so in Patrick's time funds were solicited for the
purpose of ransoming Christian slaves. We know this further
from one of the Canons attributed to a Synod of the three
Bishops, Patrick, Auxilius and Isernius: 'If a man has collected
money for captives in his community on his own, and
without permission, he deserves to be excommunicated.'
Obviously the crooked alms-collector and the phony 'benefit'
were not inventions of our times.

As a French-trained Christian bishop and head of the
Catholic Church in Ireland, Patrick conducted this business
of collecting money and buying the freedom of Christian
slaves. It will be seen from his *Confession*, too, that he was
particularly interested in the plight of converted and baptised women who, having accepted Christianity, wished

also to adopt Christian ethic and virtue, but whose bodies were subject to the will or lust of their masters.

III

THE true revelation of Patrick the man, his character, his nature, his strength as well as his fascinating human weaknesses, are to be found in that extraordinary document, the *Confessio*, written in his old age and probably not long before his death.

He stands forth as a wonderfully human being, a man with almost all man's failings, yet touched by the divine. The testimony of his own hand exposes one who is not ashamed to admit that he owed everything to God, and that, had it not been for Him, he, Patrick, would have been other than he was.

Out of the pages of the *Confessio* arises the figure of a man of indomitable purpose and compelling spiritual power, who, as Secundinus wrote in his hymn, 'in sincerity of heart had confidence in God.'

It is this sincerity, faith and confidence—the utter subjection of himself to God—that give Patrick his stature and account for the success that has placed him amongst the saints of the ages.

Patrick's trust in God breathes from every page and from every line he wrote. It replaced a confidence that he never felt in himself, for Patrick entertained no illusions as to his initial abilities and talents. But God made everything possible to him, helped him to overcome every obstacle, physical or spiritual, with which his adventurous life was studded. He walked armoured in this faith and nothing could touch him; not the swords and spears of his enemies, or the occasional envy or spite of his friends.

It was this love for God and his dedication to the life, the work and the word of Christ that gave Patrick his steadfast and unchanging nature. God was Patrick's catalyst who fused and tempered his character. From the time that the boy Patrick discovered Him on the freezing slopes of Mount Slemish, there was not a thought or action that was not first funnelled through God. Thus the Saint's line of action ran as straight as an arrow, undeviating, unwavering. It was impossible for him to act other than in concert with his God, who had called upon him to serve. He had the words of that God and that Christ, spoken through the Scriptures and the Gospels; he lived by them to the utmost of his ability and he asked of those about him and those whom he preached to and converted to try to do likewise. And you will see, glittering from some of his paragraphs like jewels, his joy when he succeeded.

There is an old Irish morning prayer known as the *Lorica*, or 'Breast-plate,' of unknown date which in the outpouring of its faith and sublime passion for the Trinity might be said to be as a crystal mirror held up before the spirit of Saint Patrick.

Indeed, there is cause to believe that he first composed and spoke some of the stanzas of this religious poem, for legend has connected him with it, and philologists have suggested that much of its structure, metre and use of words are of the sixth century, with perhaps some parts even older and reaching back another hundred years to the time of Patrick whom it so beautifully reflects.

When the High King of Tara, so the story goes, laid an ambuscade for Patrick and his companions following the defeat of the Druid Magicians and the death of the Mage Lochru on the Hill of Slane by the light of Patrick's Paschal fire, the Saint and his followers, who included the boy Benen, were in great danger of death. Patrick sang the Lorica as a breast-plate for the protection of body and soul against devils and men and vices.

Then the soldiers lying in wait looked in vain, for they saw no more than a procession of wild deer with a fawn—who was the boy Benen—moving through the forest. And from this the hymn was called 'The Deer's Cry.'

The following stanzas from this ancient poem and prayer, the words of which still ring through the cathedrals of Ireland on Saint Patrick's Day, will serve to show some of that wondrous vitality of God that burned within Patrick.

'I arise today through a mighty strength,
 The invocation of the Trinity
 Through belief in the Threeness,
 Through Confessions of the Oneness,
 Towards the Creator.

'I arise today
 Through the strength of Christ with His Baptism,
 Through the strength of His crucifixion with His Burial,
 Through the strength of His Resurrection with His
    Ascension,
 Through the strength of His descent for the Judgement
    of Doom.

'I arise today
 Through God's strength to guide me,
 God's might to uphold me,
 God's Wisdom to lead me,
 God's eye to look before me,
 God's ear to hear me,
 God's word to speak for me,
 God's hand to guard me,
 God's way to lie before me,

God's host to defend me
> against snares of devils,
> against temptations of vices,
> against the lusts of nature,
> against all who wish me harm
> from far or near,
> with few or the many.

'Christ protect me today
Against poison, against burning,
against drowning, against wounding
That I may receive abundant reward.

'Christ with me, Christ before me, Christ behind me,
Christ in me, Christ beneath me, Christ above me,
Christ on my right, Christ on my left,
Christ where I lie, Christ where I sit, Christ where I
    arise,
Christ in the heart of every man who thinks of me,
Christ in the mouth of every man who speaks to me,
Christ in every eye that sees me,
Christ in every ear that hears me.

'I arise today through a mighty strength, the
    invocation of The Trinity,
Through belief in the Threeness,
Through Confession of the Oneness
Towards the Creator.

'Salvation is of the Lord,
Salvation is of the Lord,
Salvation is of Christ.
May Thy salvation O Lord, be ever with us.'

There is a wonderful nature stanza, too, which bespeaks

more the Irish bard than the Christian Apostle, and invokes the strength of Heaven, light of the sun, brilliance of the moon, splendour of fire, speed of lightning, swiftness of wind, depth of sea, stability of earth and hardness of rock.

The prayer, which at times becomes almost an exorcism against devils, wizards and sorcerers, brims with the power of Patrick's faith. When he opened the sluice-gates and permitted the words to rush forth, idols crumbled and were washed away, demons and warlocks were swept back to the gates of Hell by the torrent.

What has it been that has led men to change faith and belief, to abandon the old gods of their forefathers, the ancient rites and beliefs, the comfortable customs that fitted them as easily as do our own thoughtless superstitions such as knocking upon wood, or blessing for a sneeze?

Why give up one set of gods or one concept for another? And how know and recognise the true God? For God was still God during all the centuries when men knew no other gods but the sun and the moon, fire and water, Venus and Priapus, trees, cats, crocodiles, blocks of stone or carved marble statuary. He was no less God, no less omnipotent, loving, all-embracing. No less did His Spirit dwell within man. All about him, man felt His power, and yet remained blind to Him.

Yet it was in the end through man that He made himself manifest. The prophets of Israel began to speak and the darkness began to lift. God had said 'Let there be light' and there was light. It was in the guise of man that Jesus appeared and gathered his disciples about him, poor, unassuming men who had in common simplicity, innocence and the ability to believe and love.

There followed then the apostles and saints and missionaries, men of faith and example spreading the concept of divinity and the story of sacrifice that moved the world. And one of these faithful, persuasive men was St Patrick.

Many and diverse factors brought about the fall of the pagan gods, but the one that stands out most powerfully was the vigour, the belief, the passionate zeal and ardency, the self-sacrifice and the glowing personalities of the men who carried the message of the Gospels.

The central and uniting theme is always sincerity. The great conversions were not made by men of sophistication or cynicism. A superlative innocence must abide in the one who stands before the multitude, or sits across the table from that symbol of human power on earth, the King, and declares, 'My God is the only true God.'

It is this stupendous innocence and sincerity that stand out in Patrick and made him what he was. His was the faith that truly was capable of moving mountains, or converting a nation, for its purity was not marred by one single solitary doubt. And it was this same sincerity and faith which impressed itself upon the Irish.

Patrick was that rarity, a staunch and good man in a wicked world, but it was his wholehearted love of God which breathes through his document which made him wish to be good, and it was by this means and along these paths that he led the Irish to accept and love that same God. For it was precisely here that the poetic beauty of Patrick's devotion appealed to the Irish heart.

The Irish understood what it was to love. Patrick was able to show them an object of adoration such as they had never encountered before, a Divinity approached by the best and highest that man had ever achieved. The manner in which Patrick the man served that Divinity, his God, reached to the poetic heart of Irish youth, for while the old kings, set in their ways, resisted, it was the princelings and the princesses,

E

according to Patrick's own telling, who first yielded to him. Patrick had the power to make Christianity in Ireland a religion for the young, the brave, the gallant and the beautiful.

And do not think that Patrick had not an eye for beauty; or, in telling the story of the high-born Irishwoman who six days after her baptism came to him with her decision to take the veil, he would not have referred to her as a blessed Irishwoman of noble birth, *beautiful*, full-grown, etc.

Patrick was no namby-pamby, impotent frustrate or neuter. He was a man from the top of his head to the tips of his toes who in the anguish of retrospect upon his life and its temptations wrote: '. . . I do not trust myself as long as I am in this body of death, for strong is he who daily strives to turn me away from the faith and the purity of true religion to which I have devoted myself to the end of my life to Christ my Lord. But the hostile flesh is ever dragging us unto death, that is, towards the forbidden satisfaction of one's desires; and I know that in part I did not lead a perfect life as did the other faithful.'

And in a sense, too, Patrick laid the beauty of this woman upon God's altar as an especial gift. It was not only the plain and the unloved who were prepared to dedicate themselves. And is there a touch of pride in the fact that this woman, whose looks, birth and position would have destined her for a different career as queen and mother, has decided to become a virgin of Christ? If so, Patrick immediately negates the flush of success. It is God's messenger who has reached her with the admonishment to renounce the world and draw nearer to Him, and it is 'thanks be to God' that she has hearkened. Nevertheless, it was the faith and sincerity of Patrick that planted in her the seed which so quickly flowered.

And in the next sentence of that paragraph—'Not that their fathers agree with them; no, they often even suffer persecution and undeserved reproaches from their parents; and yet their number is ever increasing'—we again encounter evidence of that astonishing phenomenon of the appeal of Patrick and the religion he preached to the aristocratic youth of Ireland.

When Patrick was at the height of his powers in Ireland he must have been a man of close to fifty years, yet the young followed in his train whither he went, as in the tale of the Pied Piper. He led them into continence, into scholarship, into the cold, dank cells of monasteries and the sterility of monastery life compared to the lusty existence they had been used to living. None but the most extraordinary of men could have had such an appeal.

Significant, too, it is that in all of the legend tales of Patrick's struggles with the class most bitterly opposed to him, the Druids who constituted Ireland's class of the cultured and the learned of those times, it was the poets in their ranks who succumbed most quickly to Patrick, and with some it was a case of love and understanding at first sight. The situation is too often recurrent in the legends to be wholly fabricated.

When Patrick invaded the banquet hall of the High King at Tara and Laoghaire, two men, counselled by the Druids that no one present was to stand up as a mark of respect for the Christian priests, disobeyed the order; one was Dubthach, the chief of the poets of Ireland, and the other his nephew and disciple, also a poet by the name of Fiacc.

It was Fiacc who later became one of Patrick's priests by one of those mischievous subterfuges dear to the hearts of the Irish, but wholly foreign to the nature of Patrick, who did not appear to have a sense of humour. Few truly dedicated men have.

The story as appearing in *The Tripartite Life* and elsewhere

is that Patrick plotted with Dubthach for the person of his
nephew Fiacc and, though the trick is credited to the clever
Dubthach, Patrick acquiesces in it. As the young man
approaches the two elders, the tonsuring of Dubthach seems
to be afoot in order that he may be ordained a bishop. Fiacc
protests: 'Verily, this will be a blemish to the commonwealth
[meaning that Ireland cannot afford to lose her greatest poet].
It is a grief that I am not taken in his stead.' Patrick says:
'Truly, thou wilt be taken,' and the game is over. Fiacc
is tonsured, baptised and given that most seductive and
dangerous of all weapons—the alphabet.

It has been suggested, and with considerable reason, that
one of the causes of the rapid spread of Patrick myths, and
the extraordinary nature of the personality emerging from
these legends, was that so many of Ireland's poets and literary
men were drawn into the ministry and chose it as a career
even after the passing of Patrick. The tonsure and the monk's
cowl did not put an end to their flights of imagination.

IV

PATRICK'S weaknesses were those of the modern self-made
man. He was sensitive to criticism; he was inclined to be
scornful of men of book learning, considering what he had
accomplished with so little of it; and he was disposed to be
suspicious and apparently accepted things on hearsay. The
bitterest blow of his life, his betrayal at the hands of his
dearest friend, was reported to him at second, and perhaps
even third hand, and believed. If the report was untrue—
and there is a considerable possibility that it might have been
—no man ever suffered more than Patrick for this fault.

Yet in one important factor Patrick differed from the
modern success, the fellow who has raised himself aloft by

his boot-straps. All of the credit for his achievements he ascribes to God. 'Whence I, once rustic, exiled, unlearned, who does not know how to provide for the future, this at least I know most certainly that before I was humiliated I was like a stone lying in the deep mire; and He that is mighty came and in His mercy lifted me up, and raised me aloft, and placed me on top of the wall. And therefore I ought to cry out aloud and so also render something to the Lord for His great benefits here and in eternity—benefits which the mind of men is unable to appraise.

'Wherefore, then, be astonished, ye great and little that fear God and you men of letters on your estates, listen and pore over this. Who was it roused up me, fool that I am, from the midst of those who in the eyes of men are wise and expert in law and powerful in word and in everything? And He inspired me—me the outcast of this world.'

Like the rip caused when two great ocean currents come together—the flow of the human and the divine in Patrick— one may still detect in the turmoil of those two sections of his *Confession* a touch of pardonable mortal exultation in Patrick's triumph over 'the men of letters,' and 'the wise and expert in law and powerful in word and in everything.' For they were the ones who had said all along that he would never make it, and may well have been those, too, from whom the criticism was emanating which gave rise to Patrick's defence of himself and his ministry in his document with particular emphasis on the financial side.

It would seem that Patrick's enemies overlooked no angle in their attacks upon him. He was accused of ignorance, presumption, unfitness for the job and peccadilloes with the cash box.

There is no written evidence of the accusations; we learn of them only through Patrick's vigorous defence of himself against them, and the same elements contained in the Hymn of Secundinus, for this bishop often seems to be replying to critics of his superior in his poem.

With modesty, part genuine, part attributable to the writing style of the times, Patrick acknowledges the faults with which he was born or acquired: 'I am Patrick, a sinner, most unlearned . . . I did not know true God . . . before I was able to distinguish between good and evil . . . I am imperfect in many things . . . I have not studied like the others . . . it was my sins that prevented me from fixing in my mind what before I had barely read through . . . I blush and fear exceedingly to reveal my lack of education . . . and I was not worthy, nor was I such that the Lord should grant this to His servant . . .'

Here is the humble, clear-seeing man aware of his short-comings. But fire comes into the old missionary's eye and humility no longer drips from his pen as he refutes the charges that he used his high office to enrich himself.

He tells how even at the risk of offending local *mores* as well as personal feelings he returned gifts that were offered to him by emotionally moved converts. His companions wished to accept them, but Patrick was adamant. He con-fesses that he as an individual might have been weak in this respect, but with God strong in him there could be no straying from the path.

This curious distrust of his own perhaps acquisitive nature is echoed again where he writes: 'For although I be rude in all things, *nevertheless I have tried somehow to keep myself safe*, and that too, for my Christian brethren and the Virgins of Christ.' When pious women whom he had converted, and whose living saint and object of veneration he had become, made him gifts, or laid their golden arm-bands, brooches and pins upon his altar, he returned them, 'and they were offended that I did so. But I did it for the hope of lasting success, in order to preserve myself cautiously in everything so that they might not seize upon me or the ministry of my service, under the pretext of dishonesty, and that I would not even in the smallest matter give the infidels an opportunity to defame or defile.'

What honour these scruples do the old apostle, not only for his honesty, but for his intelligence and good sense. In an era of chaos and moral decay, when every man let stick to his fingers what would, more or less, Patrick recognised what a fatal error it would be to permit the religion and the God he was preaching to be connected in any way with venality. 'Likewise as regards the heathen among whom I lived, I have kept faith with them and shall continue to do so. God knows, I have defrauded none of them, nor would I think of doing so for the sake of God and His Church . . .' The natives, apparently, were not so restricted in their dealings with Patrick in the matter of swindling, for Patrick at one point writes: 'Daily I expect murder, *fraud* or captivity.'

But it is against the charges of simony that he flames with hurt indignation: 'When I baptised so many thousands of people, did I perhaps expect from them as much as half a screpall [a small silver coin]? Tell me and I will restore it to you. Or when the Lord ordained clerics everywhere through my unworthy person and I conferred the ministry on them free, if I asked of any of them as much as the price of my shoes, speak against me and I will return it to you. On the contrary, I spent money for you that they might receive me . . .' and he continues with his accounting of how he spent the money—funds that may well have been his own rather than those of the Church, at that time—in necessary guides and escorts and protection and payments made to chieftains to gain their permission for him to proselytise in their territories.

But it is easy to read into the strange, confused prose of Patrick—the prose of the man of action rather than the writer—how the accusations rankled, and when he writes, apropos of the miracles of signs, wonders and prophecies vouchsafed him by God: 'And let those who will, laugh and scorn . . .' one can hear the scorn and laughter arising from both sides of the Channel, from the throats of jealous and cynical prelates in Britain and in France to whom the presumption and above all the fabulous success of this rude, unlearned cleric with the one-track mind was attaining were all but unbearable.

Patrick at no time trod an easy way. And the true modesty of the man is gleaned not from his professions of unworthiness and denigrations of himself, but from the manner in which he skips over the trials and hardships that beset him from his sixteenth year until the end of his days, and which he dismisses with a few words, not wishing to bore his readers.

His sensitivity to his shortcomings he sometimes offset with pride in God's sponsorship of him. In one of the strangest portions of the *Confession*, referring to that unhappy time when his candidacy for the episcopate and the title and authority of bishop was rejected by a Synod, sitting probably in Britain, he writes: 'On that day, then, when I was rejected by those referred to and mentioned above, in that night I saw a vision of the night. There was a writing void of honour against my face [condemnation]. Meanwhile I heard the anger of God saying to me: "We have seen with anger the face of the person designated"—the name being expressed— He did not say "Thou hast seen with anger," but "We have seen with anger" as if He included Himself, as He sayeth:

"He who toucheth you toucheth as it were the apple of
my eye." '

For Patrick, the dream was a pre-vision, one of those
glimpses behind the curtain granted him by God, for it
occurred on the night of the day of his rejection by the
Synod, when news of it could not possibly have reached
him, unless the meeting took place in Ireland, which from
all indications seems highly unlikely. But, perhaps, writing
in his old age of an event that took place perhaps twenty
years before, or even more, Patrick telescoped the time of
receiving the news and the night vision.

How very human psychologically is this dream following
upon a rejection by his peers and the bitter disillusionment
of his friend's action in revealing his youthful sin. Patrick
sees his own countenance and against it the 'writing without
honour,' the parchment signed by the bishops denying him
his hard won and deserved episcopate. Then he sees the face
of his friend. Patrick will not name him, but God does. And
to the unhappy, miserable, sensitive man, God reveals His
anger against this man and says in effect: 'Never mind; take
courage. I am with you. This has been done to *us*. You and
I are together in this and *I* will not let you down.'

So, indeed, Patrick took it. 'Therefore I gave him thanks
who hath strengthened me in everything . . . I rather felt
after this no little strength, and my trust was proved right
before God and men.'

V

IT was natural that Patrick, 'unlettered' and the victim of a
bad start in life education-wise, should be ill at ease and
sensitive in the presence of the most literate and educated
men of the Western world as it existed in his day—the

Catholic clergy who studied, wrote and debated in the string of monasteries and churches of southern and central France.

Just such qualities as Patrick possessed—the steadfastness of the one-track mind which knows where that track is leading to, originality, organising ability and a faith both naïve and innocent in its unquestioning devotion—could come to be despised in such literary and debating clubs where Patrick's zeal would be regarded as pushing, and his ambition to be the apostle to the Irish a kind of standing joke.

Patrick himself gives evidence of this kind of thing when he reported behind-the-back talk, which in itself must have reached him via tattlers. They were asking why does this fellow—and the very use of the word fellow indicates in some measure the contempt in which Patrick was held—throw himself into danger amongst enemies who have no knowledge of God? The question brings to mind a group of scholars and pedants who had no concept of the fires that burn in the bowels of the true missionary. The latter are a breed apart, and it is well known that the herd resents the albino.

Patrick was more charitable in his estimate of his fellows. He declared that this gossip was not malicious but merely that his ambitions did not appeal to them since they seemed to be harboured by one who was something of a clown, a rustic fellow of no book learning or background.

It would not be surprising, then, if such an atmosphere bred in him a suspicion of his fellow-men and their good intentions, a suspicion that would only grow as is the case with many self-made men who had fought their way up the ladder and left the rest of the pack far behind. For all his success, the self-made man is never sure that he is not being laughed at for some gaucherie which would not be perpetrated by some less wealthy but more cultured person. It is to disarm this laughter and scorn that Patrick throughout his vivid document refers to his rusticity and lack of learning and education, as well as poor Latin, while at the same time, the whole of it tells of one of the greatest success stories the world has ever known.

But one friend Patrick had wherever and in whatever church, monastery or school in Gaul he went to prepare himself to answer the call of the heathen Irish to walk in their midst once more. His name and person remain a mystery to which the Saint in his story provides no clue. He was older than Patrick, and unlike the others he not only befriended the ardent young man, but penetrating beneath his gauche exterior glimpsed the clear jewel that was the heart of Patrick and perhaps guessed even that he was in the presence of genius. Patrick refers to him as his dearest friend and relates that to him, in his troubled mind, he confessed to him: '. . . what I had done in my boyhood one day, nay, in one hour, because I was not yet strong. I know not, God knoweth, whether I was then fifteen years old; and I did not believe in the living God . . .'

Patrick made this confession to his friend before he had been ordained a deacon. Perhaps it was this very friend who ordained him, having assured him of forgiveness for a sin committed so long ago, so long repented, so long forgotten —Patrick then must have been thirty. The friend may well have smiled to himself, but with sympathy and under-standing for the sweetness and innocence of mind that would bring up so old a happening against his conscience and him-self. The sin itself remains a mystery. The probability, from other references of Patrick to his frequent temptations, is that it was sexual or in some way connected with carnality, and that, even in an age where people were not exactly squeamish or easily shocked, it weighed heavily on Patrick's mind.

Yet it was not so severe as to disqualify him from the priesthood; he was duly ordained a priest and, probably by the advice of his friend, the affair was put out of his mind for good—or at least so Patrick thought.

Then one day the blow fell. When and where will probably never be known. The two chronological camps are divided. Those who believe in the earlier Patrick *floruit* take it that Patrick's rejection came when he was being considered for promotion to bishop *before* going to Ireland. Those who champion the later date make it that Patrick was already functioning in Ireland as priest and missionary and that the meeting was held in Britain, or the question came up at some Synod conducted in there, as to whether his work and character warranted promoting him to bishop.

'And when I was attacked,' recounts Patrick, 'by a number of my seniors who came forth and brought up my sins against my laborious episcopate, on that day indeed was I struck so that I might have fallen for now and eternity; but the Lord graciously spared the stranger and sojourner for His name and came mightily to my help in this affliction. Verily, not slight was the shame and blame that fell upon me! I ask God that it may not be reckoned to them as a sin. As cause for proceeding against me they found—after thirty years!—a confession I had made before I was a deacon.'

Eventually word reached Patrick of what had allegedly happened at the Synod, word brought by someone who had heard it from someone else, for there is no indication that either Patrick's friend or anybody else who had been present in the Synod chamber, came to Patrick in Ireland. And Patrick, nurtured on suspicion, rebuffs and monastery intrigues, believed what he heard.

'But the more am I sorry for my dearest friend that *we had to hear* what he said. To him I confided my very soul! And I was told by some of the brethren before that defence—at which I was not present, nor was I in Britain, nor was it suggested by me—that he would stand up for me in my absence. He had even said to me in person: "Look, you should be raised to the rank of bishop!" of which I was not worthy. But whence did it come to him afterwards that he let me down before all, good and evil, and publicly, in a matter in which he had favoured me before spontaneously and gladly . . . and not he alone, but the Lord who is greater than all?'

Based upon these lines for centuries, probably not without reasonable impetus furnished by the human species, biographers have cynically taken it for granted that when Patrick's enemies in the Synod, men who would never forgive Patrick for having proven their estimates of him so wrong, opened up on him and the mood of the meeting seemed to be going against Patrick's promotion, the Saint's best friend, who had gone there avowedly to take his part and urge his episcopacy, suddenly switched, double-crossed his pupil and disciple and furnished the meeting with the necessary peg on which to hang Patrick's rejection, namely the revelation of his boyhood sin.

Yet it would appear to be too harshly cynical. What had the friend to gain from such churlish behaviour? Promotion himself? There is no indication of this. If he attended the Synod he was already a bishop. Political favour by toadying? The reward would hardly seem to fit the service which was no more than kicking a man who was already down. The manner in which Patrick speaks of this friend and the reflection we receive of the bishop's reaction to this friendship bespeak a good man and a warmth and intimacy not lightly thrown away.

Patrick had to 'hear what was said.' The hearsay brought by whom? Someone possibly jealous of Patrick's friendship with the traducing bishop? Or, more charitably, merely a bad reporter?

Since Patrick is revealed today only by interpretation, might one be permitted to imagine oneself inside the Synod chamber listening to the ardent advocacy of Patrick's friend:

'A man of pure soul and stainless heart, this Patrick,' he declares. 'There is none amongst us who loves God and Christ more or with greater passion and fervour. He is a receptacle of grace which can contain no evil. His is the sweet innocence of a child; his conscience stands guard at the portals of his spirit. Why, I recall even, when he confessed to me before ordination, that he was yet troubled by a sin committed when he was but a boy of fifteen almost two decades back . . .'

And then the rustle and stir, and the pause as the bishop broke off wishing he had not spoken. And cutting through the silence the cold voice from the hard heart: '*What* sin, my dear Bishop? Pray tell us.'

This was before the institution of private confession and the inviolability of what passed in the confessional box.

'Must I . . .? It was nothing. I was only endeavouring to show what manner of . . .'

'We command you to tell!'

And so the fat might have gone into the fire in all innocence. And not difficult for the report to reach Patrick: 'They said that it was your friend Bishop —— who told of some sin you had committed as a youth that weighted the scales against you.'

Communication was not simple in those days. There was

not a great deal of correspondence. Patrick's friend may have returned to France without ever knowing the evil report that reached the Saint in far-off Ireland. And if Patrick was guilty of a lack of faith, he was punished, for he went to his grave believing that most awful of things that can happen to humans on earth, that he had been betrayed by his best friend.

VI

IT is astonishing how few writers have made the point of Patrick's blindness to the virtues of the Irish and in particular their high culture and civilisation. It is possible that this stemmed from their having no written literature, and to a monastery-trained man, himself no great adept at the art, this may have seemed an especial benightedness.

But with Patrick's own respect for Roman law it is strange that he did not appear to be aware of the Irish nation's own high development of jurisprudence, one that in the opinion of many surpassed even the Roman, and certainly later on was of a higher order than the British. The Irish obeyed a national law that reached into the smallest and farthest Tuatha, or independent state, and had set up machinery that enabled sentences to be carried out and justice to be done no matter how complicated the suit or quarrel, or how widespread the jurisdiction. In extreme cases, the High King was empowered to intervene and execute sentence by force of arms well outside his own territory. Too, the quality of justice was restrained, civilised and intelligent.

Whereas Roman civilisation was imposed by dictatorship, and Fascism or state-ism engulfed the individual to a degree that made Mussolini's later brand seem almost enlightened liberalism, the political organisation of Ireland was democratic to a high degree: there was more individual liberty, the classes and numbers of freeholders were more extensive and, in the Tuath, embraced not only landholders, but artisans, carpenters, smiths, weavers, etc., and the professional class of teachers, poets, lawyers, doctors, etc., all of whom had an equal voice in the direction of the community. Affairs were arranged by assemblies of men of equal franchise, and governments were brought into being to serve the people, from the lowest chieftain of a small Tuath, to the High King.

This kind of enlightenment had vanished from the Continent when the light shed by Greece was extinguished a thousand years before and Rome became an empire. Yet Patrick continued to refer to these people as barbarians and savages and to bemoan his fate that it was his lot to spend his life in their midst. One of the by-products of Roman civilisation seemed to have been an arrogance that lumped every other nation and people beyond its pale as savage and barbarous, a manner of thinking that is not entirely unknown even today where for the word barbarous we substitute primitive and but recently have begun to reflect upon the propriety of the exploitation of these people beyond the outposts of our civilisation.

To Patrick the Irish remained heathens, pagans and barbarians and his two documents are filled with references to the fact that he lived amongst them only because of his love of God and his duty to win converts. Indication of friendship with non-Christian Irish may be found in the myths and legends, but none in the sole reliable source—Patrick's own words—and, reading them, one is aware of a gulf between him and the Irish that seemed bridgeable only from the moment of their acceptance of the Gospel.

He is at considerable pains to point out to his critics, even if such sentiments were not exactly flattering to the nation that was his host, that he would at all times have preferred to live elsewhere: 'On the other hand, I did not go to Ireland until I had nearly perished . . . whence was it given to me afterwards the gift so great, so salutary, to know God and to love him, although *at the price of leaving my country and my parents*. . . . How I would have loved to go to my country and my parents and also to Gaul in order to visit the brethren and to see the face of the saints of my Lord . . . likewise as regards the heathen among whom I live, I have been faithful to them. . . . I never had any reason except the gospel and its promises why I should ever return to the people from whom once before I barely escaped.'

Those who worshipped the sun—which before his coming must have taken in a good part of the Irish people, including the nobility—are characterised as 'wretches.' When longing for martyrdom, it is with 'those exiles and captives for His name' that he wishes to shed his blood. The Irish remained strangers, and their best qualities unappreciated.

But the most severe reference to his hosts through whose sufferance he was able to carry on his work is contained in the opening lines of the *Letter*, and here even Patrick realises that he is being impolite, to say the least:

'I, Patrick, a sinner, unlearned, resident in Ireland, declare myself to be a bishop. Most assuredly I believe that what I am I have received from God. And so I live among barbarians, a stranger and exile for the love of God. He is witness that this is so. Not that I wished my mouth to utter anything so hard and harsh; but I am forced by the zeal for God; and the truth of Christ has wrung it from me, out of love for my neighbours and sons for whom I gave up my country and parents and my life to the point of death. If I be worthy I live for my God to teach the heathen, even though some may despise me.'

Later in the same document he asks: 'Did I come to Ireland

without God or according to the flesh? Who compelled me? Is it of my own doing that I have holy mercy on the people who once took me captive and made away with the servants and maids of my father's house?'

Perhaps this narrow view of the people amongst whom he spent the major portion of his life was necessary to a missionary and was a part of that steadfastness of purpose that enabled him to accomplish such prodigies.

Patrick does not appear to have been a complex person or a man of great depth of intellectual attainments, and a simple division of the Irish people into pagans and non-pagans might have aided him in his work. He was not interested in them except as material for conversion, perhaps a necessary concentration. The older kings who resisted him he could see only as obstructionists and enemies and to have coddled them or made them friends would only have encouraged their intransigence.

If you wanted not to appear a barbarian in the eyes of Patrick there was but one way across the line—to believe and be baptised. To a man of Patrick's dedication there were no greys, only blacks and whites, and the blacks were very black indeed, while the whites were of that spotless purity of the soul newly won for God. In addition to which, Patrick the twig was bent into the direction of citizen of the Roman Empire with all that was implied in belonging to this great corporation. The tree never truly inclined towards the alien Irish amongst whom he lived and died an exile.

Yet there occurs in this same *Letter*, one charming, lovable and wholly human exception. In his indignation against the forces of Coroticus—the Welsh king who was nominally a Roman citizen himself—because of their attack upon the Irish coast where Patrick had apparently just held a mass baptismal ceremony, the old Apostle and Saint forgets himself. First, thundering scripture, he writes: 'The wickedness of the wicked hath prevailed over us. We have been made, as it were, strangers.' And then: 'Perhaps they do not believe that we have received one and the same baptism, or have one and the same God as father. For them it is a disgrace that we are Irish.'

We! That *we* are Irish! Here for the first and only time, Patrick identifies himself with the people amongst whom he has been living and working. If the men of Coroticus think it a disgrace to be Irish, that this is a lowly folk to be raided and slaughtered with impunity, then let them dare to include Patrick, the Romano-British Christian bishop in that estimate, for he has used the word 'we' and counted himself amongst them.

But of the warmth of Patrick's love for the baptised and converted Irish there can be no doubt. It glows through the *Confessio* and the *Letter*. They become 'neighbours'; 'sons and daughters'; 'brethren'; 'sheep of the Lord'; 'servants of Christ'; 'handmaids of Christ'; 'pious women'; 'Christian brethren'; etc.

They were in the fold. They were no longer heathens. Within them now glowed the light of that same God who was Patrick's consuming pursuit. They believed! The love of God and hence that of Patrick could embrace them. That that warmth was spread over the greater part of Ireland before the Saint laid down his crozier for the last time is indicated by his own words: 'Hence how did it come to pass in Ireland that those who never had knowledge of God, but until now always worshipped idols and impure things, have now been made a people of the Lord, and are called sons of God . . .?'

Patrick's loyalty to the Irish was twofold; one was to the barbarians whom he had pledged himself to Christ to convert and save; and the other to not only the converts he had made, but the 'exiles and captives for His name,' those Christians who had been taken there forcibly as he had been, and of whom there must have been great numbers, for in the one raid alone in which he was taken Patrick speaks of being made prisoner along with many thousands of people. It must have been these and similar slaves who were partly responsible for the introduction of Christianity into pre-Patrick Ireland to an extent where Rome thought it necessary to send a bishop to that island.

But always closest to Patrick's heart were those men, women and children of Irish birth, kings and queens, princes and princesses, Druids, lawyers, poets, teachers, warriors, craftsmen, farmers, down to the lowliest herdsmen and slaves to whom he preached the word of God and Christ and they believed. The afterglow of this love never died down over the centuries. It is reflected today in the warmth of affection which the Irish people feel for Patrick.

VII

THERE was one other thing that Patrick did for the Irish to remove them from that phase of barbarism that had earned the contempt of the so-called civilised world. He gave them the Latin alphabet. The Irish were not without writing of their own, but it was in the hands of the Druids who guarded it jealously, and their own invented alphabet, the Ogham, was used apparently only for inscriptions upon stone.

Every boy that Patrick taught, every native priest that he ordained, received an alphabet and was put to learning to read and write. Within two centuries of Patrick's coming, there had developed in Ireland a scholarship and a poetic literature unsurpassed anywhere on the Continent. Barbarism in the sense of the Roman viewpoint was at an end in Ireland, and it was Patrick who ended it. The old cultures were blended with the new. Ireland must truly have been a small piece of heaven until the coming of the Norsemen started it upon the road to destruction.

For all his steadfast devotion to his call and his unchangeful nature, Patrick was not a rigid man in that he could not take adversity or went to pieces in the face of it. His life was nothing but one long-drawn-out adventure of adversity and he could accept setbacks philosophically, or rather theologically, since whatever happened to him was God's will: 'So indeed I must accept with equanimity whatever befalls me, be it good or evil, and always give thanks to God who taught me to trust in Him always without hesitation . . .'

But this did not mean that he took trouble lying down either. He was that rare man of full religious comprehension who understood that to trust in God was not to be carried away limply by the stream or to shirk one's duties. He even acknowledges failing to heed God's signal on several occasions. God was ready: Patrick too was ready, but did not know that his time was come, that he was sufficiently prepared, and so hung back, wasting valuable time. Faith in God meant having faith in himself as well. Once he was convinced the call had come from God to take up his mission, he never wavered in that faith. His reply to his critics was less a self-searching than a 'Let's look at the record.'

Gratitude was a highly attractive facet of Patrick's character. It was directed towards God more than man since Patrick felt that it was to God rather than man that he owed everything, but to Him he released it in full flood. And it was an unusual kind of gratitude in which Patrick is thankful not for favours, or a career, or wealth poured out on him, but instead, throughout the two documents that have come down to us, is genuinely and sincerely grateful that his Creator has made it possible for him to serve Him throughout a life of hardship and danger and that God has made him the instrument to bring into the fold a people who did him a grave injury as a youth.

This feeling of gratitude leads Patrick to propound to himself an interesting theological problem. He would wish to make some return for the favours he has received: 'But what can I say or what can I promise to my Lord, as I can do nothing that He has not given me?'

Then, should there be any reward due to him for his services, there is but one thing that he asks: 'And if ever I have done any good for my God, whom I love, I beg Him to grant that I may shed my blood with those exiles and captives for His name even though I should be denied a grave, or my body be woefully torn to pieces limb by limb by hounds or wild beasts or the fowls of the air devour it.' The only return he asked for a lifetime of service was that which crowned the labours of Peter and Paul and others of the saints, captives of Christ whose lives were a model for that of Patrick.

Patrick must have been contained and reserved. It is doubtful whether any of his co-workers or disciples ever knew him really well beyond the one friend to whom he bared his soul. His love of God was an open book, but his hurts he must have kept to himself with that instinct of the leader and organiser never, if it could be avoided, to display his weaknesses.

Nevertheless he had that great human need and desire not to pass from life misunderstood and thus, before he died, he managed in spite of every handicap to put the real Patrick on paper: 'Although I am imperfect in many things, I nevertheless wish that my brethren and kinsmen should know what sort of person I am, so that they may understand my soul's desire . . .' It is also a kind of testament of encouragement to his fellow workers, for later he writes again:

'Now I have given a simple account to my brethren and fellow-servants who have believed me because of what I said and still say in order to strengthen and confirm your faith. Would that you too would strive for greater things and do better.'

Patrick was physically brave, a trait that commended him to the Irish, a nation of truculent and courageous warriors if ever there was one. It is doubtful whether tortures or indignities that were doubtless visited upon Patrick during his various captivities in Ireland ever called forth so much as a groan from his lips. It was that very fearlessness that must often have contributed to the saving of his life. Absolute, selfless courage buttressed by faith in the protection of Heaven can be upsetting to the most determined and malevolent of enemies. Many a spear-thrust missed Patrick—God's work, to be sure, but a calm and fearless eye regarding an assailant can set the steadiest hand to trembling into a miss at short range.

Filled as Patrick was with the wonder of the miracle of his life and career, he was no fool or muzzy, pious-tongued wanderer in the clouds. His feet were planted firmly on the ground; both *Letter* and *Confessio* give testimony to his political astuteness. It must have been this quality more than any other that would have been the despair of his detractors who, since they had prophesied failure and disaster for him from the outset, could not afford to wish him well. One can imagine their expressions as some itinerant cleric brought the news that still another outpost of the Irish wilderness had fallen to this rustic and unlearned bishop and someone less hostile remarked: 'Patrick has done it again!'

There was nothing supine about Patrick. He could be violently and flamingly angry and you have only to read the accusing passages of the *Letter to the Soldiers of Coroticus* to become aware of the measure of his indignation and his ability to express it: 'Dripping with blood, they welter in the blood of innocent Christians. . . . Parricide! Fratricide! Ravening wolves that eat the people of the Lord as they eat bread. . . . A murderer cannot be with Christ! . . . Who of the saints would not shudder to be merry with such persons or to enjoy a meal with them? . . . They have filled their houses with the spoils of dead Christians, they live on plunder. They do not know, the wretches, that what they offer their friends and sons as food is deadly poison, just as Eve did not understand that it was death she gave to her husband. . . . Where, then, will Coroticus with his criminals, rebels against Christ, where will they see themselves, they who distribute baptised women as prizes—for a miserable temporal kingdom which will pass away in a moment?'

Here was Patrick using the Christian weapon, moral force, against a rapacious and brutal king. Perhaps Coroticus asked mockingly when the letter was read to him: 'How many spears has this Patrick?' But the British chieftain is forgotten these fifteen hundred years and but for Patrick's letter would never have left his imprint upon history, while the Saint still lives.

Perhaps no portion of the *Confession* is more touching or grandiose in its genuine humility when Patrick's accomplishments are considered than its closing paragraph. An old and tired man has reviewed a stormy life, reliving events and emotions. Memories, ideas, associations, old hurts, old regrets have come tumbling forth in confused profusion, sometimes to the thunder of Scripture brought forth from his inexhaustible storehouse, sometimes to the sad overtones of a

human soul in pain, at others cheerful with triumph barely
disguised. He had rendered thanks to God, refuted critics,
given an accounting of his ministry, and revealed himself as
weak, sinful and human.

But in his final paragraph peace comes to the old missionary, now in his seventy-fifth or seventy-sixth year. The
storms have abated and he had brought his curragh safely to
port. Victory is his. His writing suddenly takes on a moving
clarity and style that is only dictated by the heart:

'I pray those who believe and fear God, whosoever deigns
to look at or receive this writing which Patrick, a sinner,
unlearned, has composed in Ireland, that no one should ever
say that it was my ignorance if I did or showed forth anything, however small, according to God's good pleasure;
but let this be your conclusion and let it be so thought, that,
as is the perfect truth, it was the gift of God. This is my
confession before I die.'

CHAPTER SIX

The Wells of Patrick

THE wells of St Patrick, unmarked except in the memory of the folk who live in the vicinity and the pilgrims who journey thither, lie tucked away in the soft folds of gentle hills within sight of lough, sound or sea, or rise from fissures in the rocky slopes of barren, treeless and forbidding mountains, or may be found in lush, rolling pasture lands where they green the rich grass to feed the cattle.

They are not to be discovered unaided, for they lie off the main roads concealed by thickets of thorn or the slope of a hill or a dip in a bit of farm land or meadow. Often the approach is by a road so narrow as to deny passage to a modern car. Stone fences and wooden stiles must be crossed to reach them, or lonely wastes of bog-land or mountainsides strewn with skree and pebbles.

They vary in nature in accordance with the conformation of the land where they are located. Sometimes they gush forth clear and silvery from a cleft of rock; elsewhere they may be a tiny runnel, burn or stream, or even a mere marshy spot at the bottom of a pasture where water oozes to the surface and reeds and marsh-marigold grow. They are found in the shape of the stone cylinders descending into the earth which we have come to associate with the word, as well as in their more primitive forms, hollows in the ground or a bank where living water mysteriously appears and which have been faced with stone and corbelled by the hand of most ancient man.

It is here that the presence of Patrick may be most vividly experienced in Ireland today. For these waters, God's gift, emerging from the ground played a two-fold and important part in his daily life. The crystal springs satisfied the bodily needs of himself and his adherents and disciples, quenched their thirst, cleansed their persons, filled and scoured their pots. And at other times, under the aegis of the Saint, it became the divine fluid of the rites of baptism that washed away sin and opened the gates of Heaven to the heathen.

One can understand the love that Patrick felt for wells and their vicinity.

Sites of churches founded by Patrick may be traced, since once a piece of ground has been dedicated to a religious edifice, whether originally pagan or Christian, man continues to build upon the old foundations. But not so much as a single stick of any church or building occupied by Patrick remains to us today, for they were all constructed of wood, wattles and clay and were little more than huts.

But at the wells of Patrick you may feel and say: Here Patrick stood; here he knelt; here he drank; here he prayed; here his fingers dipped into the rude font to sprinkle the rough heads of the humbly kneeling heathen whose simple and poetic souls were able to comprehend and reach for the story of the immortality of man.

Were there standing today the ruins in stone of an authenticated church of Saint Patrick, it would rest upon no firmer foundation than the traditions of the wells. For fifteen centuries have hardly altered these sources of life-giving water, or interfered with the direct memory-inheritance line of the people who dwell in their vicinity. Each generation, from the day that Patrick with relief and joy first paused at the modest fountain in their neighbourhood, has known by old man's tale or district common knowledge, or no more than absorption, that this was Patrick's well.

The well is still there where anyone can see it. Patrick paused there to refresh, to convert and to bless. Everybody knows that. What everybody knows and remembers and speaks of as though it happened yesterday is often more to be trusted than the silence of a graven stone, or an ancient bit of wall or foundation. These *were* Patrick's wells. It is there that you will still find him.

Mearne Well is located close to Saul, in County Down, that Saul of Dichu's Barn, that gift of the Irish chieftain to Patrick that became the Saint's first church in Ireland. From the little grotto where the water emerges from the ground, a space no more than eight feet across, flows the stream of Mearne, very likely in the age of Patrick a rivulet that formed a boundary between the domains of Dichu and the neighbouring kinglet.

It takes a keen eye to detect the slight break in the hedge on the road from Downpatrick to Saul where one climbs over a broken stone fence on to a narrow cobbled path leading through oak shrub and undergrowth to the well of Mearne.

Already yards before reaching it, the stones of the path turn wet and slippery denoting the presence of water. You come then upon the little grotto itself set into the side of the hill, in the shape of half of a beehive.

Its sides consist of ancient Celtic stonework, blocks of dressed field stone set brickwork-fashion without mortar or any kind of binding, and the well was once corbelled in the fashion of southern Spain, once a centre of Celtic culture. Dressed stone is field rock that has been chipped, shaped and hand-trimmed to fit tightly. Corbel work refers to the covering of the opening at the top of a well or spring with flat slab stones to keep out debris. There are still pieces of corbel stone lying about the well of Mearne. They have been lying there untouched for centuries. Once the hands of Patrick must have rested upon them.

Slightly to the left of the well there is, embedded in the bank, a large stone hollowed out to form a kind of miniature basin. Here legend has curiously closed its eyes to its functional use, but yet has endowed it with something of the sanctity inherent in it. It is supposed to mark the spot where Patrick knelt, and the hollow is the impression of the knee of the Saint.

The stone is in all probability a primitive baptismal font and surely was used by Patrick for that purpose. Another similar stone is to be seen on the altar of the ruins of one of the earliest stone Christian churches on the island of Inchagoill in Loch Corrib, that *Inis an Ghaill Cràibhthigh*, 'The Island of the Devout Foreigner,' he being Lugnaid, the pilot-navigator nephew of St Patrick who lies buried in the ancient graveyard there beneath an inscribed stone shaped like a ship's rudder and rudder post.

Legend, too, has touched this font. The story is that it is never without water in its hollow, no matter how long a drought has kept rain from falling into the roofless ruin.

Still another such font stone is in private hands, having been found used as part of a field wall not far from Downpatrick.

In and about the well of Mearne there is the soft murmur of water breaking the silence of the leafy dell. This was the neighbourhood both written of and remembered as the location of the beginning of Patrick's work in Ireland and here it was that he made his first converts. Such are the tenderness and seclusion of the spot that one is easily pervaded with a sense of mysticism; standing in this most likely sanctuary of Patrick, it is not difficult to picture and be touched by the exultation that must have filled his heart almost to bursting as at last he realised that heart's desire to lead the unbaptised Irish from the darkness and confusion of paganism to the light and comfort of his deeply cherished Christianity.

Once this glade was, like Patrick, a-tremble with fervour, the love of humans for God and His children; it rang with the joy of salvation; here were harvested the first fruits of the near-life-long sowing of this devout, unswerving and stead-fast man. The sweet waters of Mearne delivered the souls of the lost and wandering into safe harbour. The faint echoes of this Divine and human collaboration still hover about the well.

Near Raholp, close to Strangford Lough, the site of Patrick's landing-place in Antrim, are the wells of Struell, the Drinking Well and the Eye Well, and here the sailors of Patrick replenished the ship's butts. The Saint and his party drank the clear, cool water and gave thanks to God. As it was then, the water is today, cold, fresh and sweet, but the use made by Patrick of these wells has endowed them with sanctity and the powers of healing.

They stand almost side by side on the floor of a green, hidden-away meadow, sunken, stone-lined wells, corbelled, or roofed over. The Drinking Well is beehive-shaped, the Eye Well has a peaked roof. There is not the same feeling of presence as there is about the Fountain of Mearne, yet a tree close to the Drinking Well bore unusual fruit, a piece of a crutch, and bits of rag fastened to the branches, in testimony of the miracles of healing that had taken place there in St Patrick's name. Drinking of the waters that had once slaked the thirst of the missionary and his crew had enabled the halt and the lame to walk. The waters of the Eye Well were no longer for drinking, but to help the blind once more to see. Legend and faith had endowed this spring with curative properties for diseases of the eye.

At Armagh, supposed seat of Patrick's Episcopal See, near to the ringed fort and fosse of Navan where once the queens of Macha ruled, there is yet another Well of St Patrick, reached by climbing a stile to walk the slope of a piece of pasturage slanting down to the overgrown remains of an ancient road known as the 'Green Road' which led from Tara to the fortress of Ard Macha.

If Patrick came to Armagh, this road, now a dark tunnel leading to the Callan River and overgrown with trees and shrubs, knew the grinding of the wheels of his chariot. If he took that road, he would have stopped at the well on the side of the hill and made it his.

Legend and faith again have declared that this is so and that once a year the well overflows. On the Eve of the Feast of St Peter and St Paul there is an annual pilgrimage to this spot.

Enchantment is woven about this little hillside pool today. The water is muddied by the lazy, sad-eyed cattle who pasture and drink there, but there is a great, crooked fairy thorn that grows from the spring, its roots literally cradling the waters like a chalice. The branches of the thorn tree are laced with the hundreds of wisps of cloth left there by the pilgrims in almost a return to the fetichism of paganism.

There are a simplicity and a power about this spot that evokes thoughts of St Patrick, that man of power and simplicity. It is nothing, a little muddied pool rising in a hillside. And yet it is everything, and one is loath to leave there.

It is a curious fact that for all of the great love of Patrick alive in Ireland today, not a single one of these secluded, natural temples, the wells and baptismal fonts of Patrick, the sward trod by his feet, the sites looked upon by his eyes and the waters made holy by their use in the baptism and clarification of human souls, are map-marked or sign-posted.

Were you to walk in Antrim or Roscommon, Galway or Donegal, you might drop your knapsack and stretch out to rest by some quiet meadow spring, or fill your flask at the gush of some cold, sparkling waters emerging from clefts in the grey rock and feel no more than the peace of the spot and the moment with perhaps gratitude for the gift of drink, and never know that Patrick had been there before you, cupping his work-worn hands to the flow and blessing the God whose manifestation and creation it was.

Indeed, without the aid of someone who lived near there and who shared in the heritage memory of the neighbourhood, you would never find a single one of these places that alone in Ireland today still physically remain as they were when Patrick came and rested, preached and baptised there.

Journey in County Roscommon from Boyle to Frenchpark, thence south through Bellanagare to Tulsk—a trip that crosses a great plain rich in cattle-fattening grass, a rolling country of low ridges, long gradual slopes and swelling mounds, deceptive in their height—there is nothing to tell you that you are crossing the ancient plains of Magh Ai, that you are within sight and reach of the great burial grounds of the Irish kings and Rathcroghan, the palace fortress of the legendary Queen Maeve.

Your eye may be caught by a solitary monolith against the skyline atop a mound to the right of the road, a pillar of red sandstone, the last, lonely sentinel guarding the remains of the early rulers of Ireland, many of whose lives were bound up with the life and person of St Patrick.

Legend and semi-history has it that the pillar marks the

resting-place of Dathi, the successor and nephew of King Niall, that same Niall of the Nine Hostages, the famous sea ruler whose raiders may have been involved in the kidnapping of Patrick when he was a boy. Dathi was one of the first, but not last, Irishmen to die fighting in a foreign war. He was thought to have fallen in what is now Switzerland, as a Roman auxiliary, in the struggle against the Franks.

To the north of Dathi's pillar is Cruachan, or Rath-Croghan, a powerful fort and in Patrick's time the stronghold of one of the Kings of Connacht. From its rounded eminence today one can still see, on the shape of lesser mounds, the ring of outlying and screening fortresses that protected the great Rath.

To the west of this mound on a back road is another of those innocent springs that bear the name 'St Patrick's Well.' But it is to the east of the fort, a half-mile down the slope or so, and impossible to find without the aid of a native of the district who is also something of an antiquarian, where lies the Fountain of Clebach, one of the most famous of all of the springs in Ireland connected with the Saint.

For it is at the Fountain of Clebach that some early Christian-Irish poet and hagiographer sets the strange story of the catechism, baptism and death of the two lovely Irish princesses, Ethne the blonde and Fedelm of the fiery tresses, daughters of Laoghaire, High King of Ireland, as the result of meeting there with Patrick and his accompanying ecclesiastics.

Clebach today is a wet spot on a bit of farmland near the bottom of the long slope of Cruachan, reached by a laborious walk crossing many stiles, ditches and stone walls across meadows where fat cattle and sheep graze contentedly, until quite suddenly the meadow is no more, but is replaced by spongy turf that soon turns into an area of small springs

F

coming up out of the ground. Reeds, marsh-flag and marsh marigolds grow here and the cattle come to drink, stepping cautiously on the soft ground.

Just above the waters, on a piece of level, solid ground, you will find the ruins—no more than the outline of the foundations and walls of a small, early Christian church that in all probability, several centuries after the death of St Patrick, was erected upon the site of the original little church built of clay which the missionary established on that site. With all the water abundant in Ireland in the form of burns, rivers and the wondrous blue lakes, it seemed to be the lavish and mysterious springs that merged from the earth that Patrick loved the most.

The story, then, is told of Patrick, with his bishops and clerics, repairing one morning to the Fountain of Clebach on the meadow-green slope of Rath Croghan before sunrise to meditate and pray.

They were tonsured after the Christian fashion, garbed in white. And a strange sight they must have presented to the two princesses, one with hair so pale that it was almost white, the other swinging two braids of copper hue, as at sunrise they came, as was their custom, to the fountain for their morning wash.

The princesses looked upon Patrick and his clerics with awe and wonder and queried them without fear whether they were of the *Sidhe*, the fairy folk who lived beneath the earth, or the equally legendary Tuatha De Danann, people of the Goddess Danann supposed at one time to have colonised Ireland. Or were they phantoms or illusions? They asked: 'Whence have ye come and where is your home?'

With a strange severity, Patrick replied: 'It were better for you to believe in the true God whom we worship than to ask questions about our race.'

The girls then asked about this God, and Patrick expounded his creed, asking the girls to believe. Catechising them further, he prepared them for baptism which they accepted, and the ceremony took place there at the fountain with the waters of Clebach. Their foreheads were anointed with chrism, and a white veil was placed over their heads.

Then, so runs the narrative in the *Tripartite Life of St Patrick*, '. . . they asked to see Christ face to face. And Patrick said to them: "Ye cannot see Christ unless ye first taste of death and unless ye receive Christ's body and His blood." And the girls answered: "Give us the sacrifice that we may be able to see the spouse." Then they received the Eucharist and fell asleep in death; and Patrick put them under one mantle in one bed; and their friends bewailed them greatly.'

Later, the guardians of the little princesses appear, two Druids by the name of Mael and Caplait. At first they contend with Patrick, but later are converted and tonsured and join those mourning at the bier of the girls who are buried by the fountain and have a tomb erected over them. The territory of Magh Ai was given to Patrick in perpetuity and the Saint erected a church by the grave of the sisters. Later, their remains were removed to Armagh to await the Resurrection.

It is a strange story, compounded of fact and pious fiction, the fact being that the tomb of the two princesses was known and remembered as being by the Fountain of Clebach more than a century after the passing of Patrick. A Patrician church was founded and built there by the well, and on its site rose a later Christian church of stone.

The fiction is evident in the fact that nothing that is supposed to have taken place there that fatal morning is consonant with the real Patrick, the Patrick of the *Confessio*, the humble, loving man and not at all the stern, arrogant inquisitor who helped two innocent young girls to their untimely end.

Every line of Patrick's references to his converts breathes love, pity and understanding. He sought to win virgins to Christ but only in the monastic sense in that many of his converts became the forerunners of nuns, eschewed marriage, vowed chastity and devoted their lives to the church.

It was Archbishop Healy of Tuam, himself the writer of a great biography of St Patrick, who set forth a test for the many legends and apocryphal stories ascribed to Patrick—do they conform to the Patrick self-revealed in his *Confession?* If not, they must be rejected as inventions.

The truth of what actually transpired by the well of Clebach will never be known, how the princesses met their death, whether they were ill and Patrick won them to Heaven by baptising them before their deaths, or whether they ever met the Saint at all. Perhaps it was that very nobly born Irish woman of whom Patrick writes, princess or queen from King Amolngaid's Rath atop the hill, who was baptised by him where the waters of Clebach welled from the soil, and whose decision to live as a virgin of Christ became confused with the story of the two princesses.

It is not difficult to place Patrick there at some period of his travels through Ireland. The Fountain of Clebach lay across his path through the west where the ruins of the later church are still to be seen, just as the ruins of many churches throughout Ireland known to have been built upon the site of original Patrician churches, still survive.

But it is the murmuring, or the whispering, or the rushing, tumbling and shouting of the waters springing from the ground that today speak the loudest and most movingly of the physical and spiritual presence of the Saint.

CHAPTER SEVEN

The Mountains of Patrick

DOWN through the ages the face of the earth changes. Forests disappear or are consumed by man. Rivers alter their courses. The sea recedes from or encroaches upon the coastline. Alone, natural springs, wells, water sources and mountains seem to resist the weight of the centuries.

In Jerusalem there is water in the Fountain of Gihon and the Pool of Siloam; the wells of Abraham flourish again in the Negeb; the fountains where Jesus rested and drank still flow; the River Jordan still gushes from oleander-lined clefts and caves near Baniya and Dan on the slopes of Hermon, as it did in the days of the kings. So we have seen, too, that the water sources and wells of Ireland have remained substantially as they were in the days, fifteen hundred years ago, when Patrick refreshed himself, prayed and baptised by their waters.

Mountains likewise resist the years. It takes an age of ten million years rather than a few dozen centuries before erosion changes their contours. The shores of the Lake of Galilee have altered since the time of Jesus, but not the mountains upon the slopes of which he preached or meditated. The peaks of Canaan and Tabor are the same today as when the eyes of the Lord looked upon them.

There are two mountains in Ireland that played an important part in the life of St Patrick, two isolated peaks, strangely and more than coincidentally similar in shape, not connected with any chain, one on the east coast, the other on the west, rising starkly from the plain. They are today exactly as they were when Patrick knew them. On the slopes of one, Mount Slemish, Patrick the boy slave once herded sheep and swine for a master. On the peak of the other, Mount Aigli, now Croagh Patrick, he may well have retired to meditate.

It is a curious feature of both these mountains when approached from the south that each resembles a cone or pyramid, each has a small extension or fore-peak, and each, when one approaches more closely and finds oneself alongside it, changes its aspect to a kind of round, hump-backed mountain, something like an inverted bowl, though Croagh Patrick remains more pointed at the top than Slemish, and is slightly more than a thousand feet higher.

Mount Slemish, *Sliabh Miss*, is located in the valley of the Braid, in Antrim in Northern Ireland. This was the ancient Ulidia then divided into Dal-riada to the north and Dal-aradia to the south, and Mount Miss as it was then called, *Sliabh* or *Slieve* being the Gaelic for 'Mount,' was in northern Dal-aradia.

Roughly the mountain lies close to the centre of a triangle formed by the inland centre of Ballymena and the two coastal towns of Glenarm and Larne. At Larne there is the narrow entrance to a sheltered sea lake, Lough Larne, formed by the seven-mile-long peninsula known as Island Magee, though it is no island at all. Lough Larne, it will be seen at a glance, provides ideal harbourage for fleets of small sail and curraghs —ships of hide stretched over wickerwork frames, such as were used by the Irish sea raiders in the time of Niall of the Nine Hostages.

The fore-hill of Slemish, which, when viewed from the

side, is seen to be a part of it, is known as Skerry, and here
was located the *dun* or fortress house of the Pictish chieftain
Miliucc, the master to whom Patrick was sold as a slave.
Slemish itself rises 1,437 feet from a barren and desolate
moor. It is treeless as are all of the mountains of Ireland above
a thousand feet. Yet there are green patches to relieve the
mottled grey rock that reach almost to the top where from
the north the outline of the formation known as Patrick's
Chair may be seen. Field-glasses resolve the moving white
dots upon these green patches into sheep grazing there, the
descendants of the animals that Patrick herded there, perhaps.

To the east of the mountain the desolate land improves to
support farms and farmhouses. In Patrick's time this area,
including the hill of Skerry, was heavily wooded. In fact,
the greatest physical change that has come to Ireland in the
past fifteen hundred to two thousand years is the disap-
pearance of the great forests that once grew there. The grim,
bare, lonely hills of Connemara, in the west wind-swept and
rock-strewn, an endless vista of melancholy not unlike the
naked mountains of Moab, were once rich and green with
tall trees. In Ireland as well as in the Holy land the naked
hills today mark the greed and destructive thoughtlessness
of man.

At one time these woods stretched from square-shaped
inland Lough Neagh to the sea. Indeed, remnants of these
may be seen to the east of Slemish on the road from Ballymena
to Glenarm where the eastern slopes of the valley are still
heavily wooded.

These, and the forests that once surrounded the base of
Slemish, were the forests of the Ulaidh, the *Siluam Uliti* of
the original manuscript of Patrick's confession, later misread,
garbled and mis-copied, according to the late Prof. Eoin
MacNeill, to read *Siluam Focluti*, and touch off a controversy

that still rages as to the exact location of Patrick's slave years and the woods from which the call of the children of Ireland came to him in a dream in later years begging him to return to them and walk in their midst once more.

For, oddly, there *was* a Sylva Focluti in Ireland in Patrick's day, located near Killala in Northern Tirawley, where Patrick founded a church, and stretching west into Mayo to the foot of that other mountain dedicated to the Saint, Sliabh Aigli, now known as Croagh Patrick.

It was on the harsh, chill, wind- and rain-swept crest of Slemish that Patrick found the presence, comfort and the love of God, just as it was to the still higher peak of Aigli that he went to communicate with Him.

The mountain has always been man's stairway to God. Stand upon the summit of Mount Canaan between Galilee and the sea at night when the heavens curve downwards and the stars may be touched . . . and the feeling of the Presence is unmistakable.

It was on the slopes of Slemish that God first spoke to Patrick.

Here it was that for six years, from the age of sixteen to twenty-two, Patrick the slave tended the swine of Miliucc in the forests where they fed on acorns or rooted beneath the moss. At other times, he took the sheep to the high pastures atop of Slemish and herded them there in wind and weather.

Look upon Slemish today and you can grasp something of the ordeal of a lonely boy snatched from loving and indulgent parents and a life of ease and luxury to the rigours of slavery, exile and abuse. For Slemish is in itself a lonely mountain standing in isolation in the plain like an island rising from the ocean. Its brow caught the brunt of the storms whirling in from the sea, the driving rains and snows, the cold mists and fogs, with not so much as a sapling beneath which to shelter.

It was during these six years and upon this mountain that the character of Patrick was formed. The iron went into his body as the Spirit entered into his soul. Here he acquired the hardy frame and physical endurance that were to see him through his missionary years in Ireland. Here he suffered spiritually and bodily until he could suffer no more, until there was no more that life could do to him that it had not done.

Out of the fires of this crucible came the courage of one who has nothing further to fear from man or beast. Here despair was conquered and steadfastness and indomitable purpose were born, the limits of human endurance learned.

Here too he came to that faith in God, that belief in His concern for him, and that love for Him, that were to become his guide and support to the end of his days.

You cannot see the place where the infant Patrick first saw the light of day, for no one can point out the spot or name it, and no two scholars agree where it might have been, but when you gaze upon Slemish you are in the presence of the site where Patrick the man and the Apostle of Ireland was born out of the chrysalis of Patrick, the indolent, sinful boy.

You may, if you will, stand upon the very ground where took place the transformation that was to alter the course of a nation and, in some instances, the world itself; when the fires of Christianity kindled by Patrick in Ireland became beacons in the darkness as the barbarian invasions threatened to extinguish the light on the continent of Europe.

It was of this sojourn that he himself wrote in his *Confessio:* 'Now, after I came to Ireland, tending flocks was my occupation and many times a day I prayed . . . the love of God and

His fear came to me more and more and my faith was strengthened. And my spirit was moved so that in a single day I would say as many as a hundred prayers and almost as many in the night, and this even when I was staying in the woods and on the mountain. And I used to get up for prayer before daylight, through snow, through frost, through rain, and I felt no harm and there was no sloth in me . . . as I now see, because the spirit within me was then fervent.'

And on the lonely mountain top God's voice could be heard more clearly.

It was on, in and about Slemish and Skerry that Patrick acquired the practical education that in later years fitted him particularly for his mission to the pagan Irish. For it was here he learned their language, beliefs, customs, politics, laws and organisation. He became acquainted with their culture, characteristics, poetry, government, their strength and their weaknesses, and it was in these formative years that he learned to deal with the Irish.

It was on the approaches to Skerry likewise, and within sight of the Slemish of so many painful as well as sweet memories, that Patrick in later life upon his return to Ireland experienced a deep human tragedy and an affecting rejection, if there is more than the usual single kernel of truth in the legend connected with that return.

It is told that shortly after his landing in Ireland, in the vicinity of Strangford Lough and what is now Downpatrick, the Saint journeyed north to pay a visit to Miliucc, his old master, with a twofold purpose, both of which were characteristic of Patrick. He wished to pay off his debt to Miliucc in money, for Patrick never questioned slavery as an institution or a way of life in his times, and, when he had made his escape, he was well aware that he was robbing his master of a valuable piece of property which he had purchased at full price. It was this price that Patrick would have been eager to restore.

And then he desired to make one who by then must have been an old man his convert and rescue his soul before his death. However hard a lord Miliucc might have been, Patrick felt affection for him. The years that had intervened would have softened the memories of harshness, and left him with the same eagerness and excitement to see this man once again, as we are thrilled and excited over the prospect of returning to our old school after a long absence to hob-nob generously with the stern schoolmaster whom we once feared and perhaps even hated.

But Miliucc, according to the legend, was stubborn, hard-headed and intransigent. For reasons of his own he did not wish to face his former slave now returned as a dignitary of a new religion. It would not have been a guilty conscience, since no one felt guilty about slavery in those times, for there was no place or country in the world where it did not exist. Perhaps he was afraid that Patrick would convert him.

His reaction was drastic. According to the story he shut himself up in his Dun with all his treasure and personal belongings, kindled a fire and immolated himself.

The chronicler who wrote this tale 1,300 years ago narrates: 'Then Patrick stood still on the southern side of Slemish—there stands a cross in that place—and he saw the fire from afar. He was silent for the space of two or three hours except for sighing and groaning. Then he said: "I know not, God knows. Yonder Miliucc's house is on fire. He is burning himself lest he believe in the Eternal God at the end of his life. Upon him lies a curse: Of him shall be neither king nor crown prince and in bondage will his off-spring and his seed abide for ever, and his soul shall not come out of hell up to doom after doom."'

This is not any Patrick that we know who would have pronounced such a curse upon the father of children who, according to other stories, were his friends and later his converts. Rather one can see him standing there, silently weeping, before turning away to blame himself and his inadequacy for this tragedy, a soul lost through some fault or weakness of his own.

The slopes and vicinity of Slemish, then, are richer in the presence and tradition of Patrick than almost any other spot in Ireland. Yet there is no shrine there, marker or tablet, not even one of those appalling white statues of studied anachronism supposed to represent this remarkable man.

These are reserved by fact and tradition to the second mountain in Patrick's life in Ireland, the one ascending 2,510 feet in Western Mayo, known as Croagh Aigli when first Patrick's eyes rested upon it, and, from then onwards and for ever after, as Croagh Patrick.

Croagh Patrick rises from the bleak moors of Murrisk between Westport and Lewisburgh by the side of Clew Bay. The view from its summit on a clear day can move one to tears if one is moved by beauty. To the north-east the ultra-marine of Clew Bay is dotted with dark-green islets, yielding then to the lighter meadow green of Irish coastland. Across Clew Bay are the purple hills of Burrishoole, Erris and the Curraun Peninsula, like amethyst rising out of a setting of emeralds rimmed with the lapis lazuli of the sea. The clouds that ever seem to wander across the face of Ireland change the colours on the hills from the light lavender of heather to deep mauve, rain-grey or dusk-blue.

To the west beyond Clare and Achille Islands sparkles the Atlantic Ocean, while eastwards, as though imitating the waves of the sea, roll the swells of the bogs of the plains of Mayo. Southwards stretches the loneliness of the tarns until the eye is caught by the peaks of the mountains of Mweelra and Partry.

But it is the coastal indentations of Ireland that are so breath-taking in their beauty and once seen, never forgotten, for the blue of the sea and the green of the land are special in their shades and contrast, like none other in the world, and the Irish sky has a depth and colour of its own that reach to the heart. From the summit of the mountain one can breathe in this beauty in great draughts, and then, or in the night when the stars came out and down almost to powder one's shoulders and reflect from the waters of the bay so that one seems almost imprisoned between stars and stars, one's thoughts would turn, as Patrick's did, inevitably to God.

Birds are mentioned in the legend of Patrick contending with the angel atop of Aigli for the right to release the souls of the Irish from Hell, black birds and white, and the song of the white birds was heavenly. The birds, of course, were crows, jackdaws and perhaps starlings for the black; gulls for the white. If you have been brought up by the sea, if you love the sea and all that is in and about it, sometimes there can be no sweeter music or more nostalgic than the soft crying of the gulls.

The approach to Croagh Patrick from the road is almost shockingly prosaic. Just past Murrisk there is a longish, narrow and somewhat battered pub called 'Patrick Campbell's Hotel' and just beyond it, a small, red-painted sign—'TO CROAGHPATRICK'—points to a footpath that turns into a stony road, such as one might expect to encounter in purgatory, leading to the base of the dark mountain whose face is scarred by the white cicatrix of the way that leads to the top.

It is barren and sad at the base of the mountain, with not a tree in sight. On a rise stands the white marble statue of the Saint in mitre, chasuble and crozier, venerably bearded which he in all likelihood was not. The path winds past huge, tumbled blocks of stone to where the mountain rises abruptly from the plain.

'And Patrick,' chronicled Tirechàn, one of the Saint's earliest biographers, 'journeyed to Mount Aigli to fast on it forty days and forty nights, observing the discipline of Moses, Elijah and of Christ. And his driver died in Murrisk Aigli, that is the plain between the sea and Mount Aigli. And he buried Totmael the driver and he heaped stones around his tomb and he said, "May it remain so for ever. And it shall be visited by me in the last days."'

So Patrick was mourning when first he climbed Mount Aigli, and this perhaps was amongst the reasons why he needed retreat and meditation. There was always a bond between Patrick and his charioteers, for the Saint himself was an able man with the reins. There is the story of how one of these drivers gave his life for Patrick. Apprised of a plot to kill him, he persuaded the Bishop to change places with him so that Patrick was driving and he occupying the single seat behind to take the spear intended for his master in his own body.

Patrick was in Mayo, preaching, converting, baptising, founding churches. He founded a church at Aghagower, and from there the sharp-pointed pyramid of The Reek, as Mount Aigli was also known, was plainly to be seen, a beckoning stairway to God for whom Patrick had been labouring long and arduously. The Saint needed to talk with Him, to hear His voice again in encouragement and approval. It had been on a not dissimilar mountain, the far-off Slieve Miss of his boyhood captivity, where God's voice and messages had first reached his inner ears. Croagh Aigli must have drawn him like a magnet.

But Patrick left another monument behind him on Aigli besides the white marble that adds nothing to the bleak approach. Each July, hundreds upon hundreds of the faithful make a difficult pilgrimage to the summit of Croagh Patrick where there is a small chapel and oratory. They start from the bottom in the dark of the early hours of the morning and scramble up a narrow path, a long and arduous climb made even more difficult by the uncertain footing and loose stones.

They make the pilgrimage to walk where Patrick walked, to be where Patrick was, to see what Patrick saw, and, if they can find the humility in their hearts, and the genuine need and love of God, to feel what Patrick felt.

For, as has been written, the mountains do not alter, and this great stone stood sentinel over the blue bay in Patrick's time. There the climbers meet at once God and His Apostle Patrick, for it was this dedicated man's devotion to the Irish that had brought him the wearisome way to this summit to refresh himself spiritually at the fountain of his faith in order that he might find the strength the better to carry on his tasks, labours that he describes himself in his *Confessio:*

'. . . wherever I journeyed for your sake through many perils, even to the farthest districts, beyond which there lived nobody and where nobody had ever come to baptise, or ordain clergy, or to confirm the people. With the grace of the Lord, I did everything lovingly and gladly for your salvation.'

Outlying districts beyond which lived no one—the very edge of the Western Sea, and even beyond, for the tales in Mayo have Patrick embarking in a curragh from the beach where the land comes to an end below Carrickyvegraly Point and breasting the long Atlantic rollers to visit tiny Caher Island between Clare and Inishturk, to carry the word to the few wild and hardy heathens who clung to this rock to eke fish from the sea. And beyond that there lived no one, or Patrick would not have turned back.

The Mountains of Miss and Aigli have looked upon the labours of Patrick and, too, upon Patrick himself, the steadfast man.

CHAPTER EIGHT

The Journeys of Patrick

I

THE missionary journeys of Patrick embraced almost the whole of Ireland, with the possible exception of that western portion between Galway and Limerick, and also the south-western tip.

His routes, the districts, regions, kingdoms, duns, raths and palace fortresses—since there were no cities, towns or even villages in Ireland in Patrick's time—he visited and the churches he founded have survived in the Memoirs of Bishop Tirechàn, writing in the eighth century a collection of notes on Patrick's travels, and in local legend.

There is hardly any portion of Ireland where you will not encounter a Patrick's Well, or a Crosspatrick, or some local derivation commemorating the passage of the Saint, or his pausing to convert, baptise, or found one of his primitive wooden-hut or wattle-and-clay churches.

Some of these landmarks are surely of later origin, invented to enable the residents to share in the renown of Patrick and the glory of having been amongst those who recognised his sainthood and succumbed to his preaching. But for the most part they do reflect a visit from the great Apostle.

All of the place-names, almost, recorded by Tirechàn, as well as those in the collection known as *The Tripartite Life* have changed, or altered their spelling, or been anglicised, or in many cases have vanished altogether. They are today no more than mounds or swellings in the landscape in the vicinity of Patrick country, or a spring, ford, or bend of a river remembered, so that only an antiquarian-geographer-philologist-archæologist-cum scholar can successfully trace the criss-crosses of Patrick's comings and goings and the sites of his churches.

Not one of these buildings of perishable material, of course, remains today. On some of these sites were later Christian churches of stone, now in ruins, or almost entirely obliterated by the storms of centuries of conquest, reformation and persecution that swept over Catholic Ireland. Others can only be guessed at. But the numbers run literally into the hundreds, and the net that Apostolic fisherman Patrick cast, to use his own favourite simile, covered almost all of the important places of then civilised Ireland, and stretched even to those furthermost places where no one had ever gone before to baptise and ordain clerics—places beyond which, in the words of the Saint, no man lived.

But, in the main, the larger districts and divisions of Ireland, Ulster, Connacht, Meath, Donegal, Roscommon, Antrim, Leinster, Munster, Sligo, existed somewhat as today, some originally as Tuaths or independent states such as the territory of Dichu in Dalaradia, others as federations of Tuaths amalgamated into one of five main groups known as Fifths, or *Coiced*, such as Connacht.

In the main, Patrick in his organisation of his Irish church used the Tuath and its extent as the boundary for a parish or diocese, and arranged for the episcopal sees to be located close to the palace fortress indicative of a king with jurisdiction over an amalgamation of a number of Tuaths. After negotiating with the petty king or chief for a grant of land, Patrick established his churches or the beginning of a monastic order or grouping, saw to the selection, education and

ordination of a native clergy to staff it, each time forging
another strong link in an organised church that has with-
stood the buffeting of fifteen centuries and its attendant
changes on the mind and soul of man.

It is impossible to estimate the number of miles travelled
by Patrick during the twenty-five to thirty years of his work
in Ireland but, if his trek on foot from Mt Slemish to Wicklow at the time of his escape logged close to 200 miles, his
peregrinations in and about Ireland must have run into tens
of thousands.

A few of his trips he was able to make through coastal
waters, but the majority of distances covered were by chariot
or ox-drawn cart or on foot. There were no Roman roads
in Ireland, only what amounted to rough tracks through
forest and over the seemingly endless miles of bog-land.
There were no bridges. Rivers were crossed at fords. There
were no towns to offer hospitable lodging, no relays, changes
of horses, no shelter from wind, rain, hail and lightning
unless the travellers happened to be near the hut of some
farmer or the larger stockade of a nobleman or chief who,
the chances were, would probably be hostile or unfriendly
to Patrick and his party.

According to *The Tripartite Life* and other sources which
credit Patrick with coming to Ireland in 432 hard upon the
heels of the mysteriously vanished Palladius, and as a fully
accredited bishop of the Gallic church, Patrick travelled in
considerable caravan, with cooks, herders, artificers, carpenters, smiths, clerics, a strong-man or personal bodyguard,
and even a handful of women who sewed vestments and
embroidered altar cloths and linens for the newly-founded
churches. Added to this were the youngsters whom he was
teaching and training, and probably hangers-on in the shape

of self-appointed assistants to the Saint, or converts drawn by his magnetic personality.

Such safaris were expensive and necessarily slow. Material had to be carried such as iron and bronze, cloth and food and drink. Fuel was supplied by the flooring of Ireland, the peat bogs. The bank account would have gone along as well, but under its own power, since it would have been cows, the medium of value and exchange in the Ireland of Patrick's time. And Patrick's retinue included a cowherd.

If, however, the later chronologists are correct and Patrick was priest and missionary in Ireland before he became bishop and ruler of the church, it is probable that he moved in lighter train at first and more quickly, seated to the right of and behind the charioteer who drove him. The chariots were springless, the tracks rough. There is no evidence that Patrick's travels were seasonal. The heathen were many and the span allotted to man to do his work was short. Spring, summer, autumn and winter must have seen Patrick abroad on the never-ending rounds of his self-imposed exile.

Patrick's eyes seemed almost always bent towards Heaven but, whenever they were able to spare a glance round and about him, he must have noted that he was travelling through an earthly paradise.

Land, water and sky in Ireland combine to make a palette of colours unsurpassed. They do not consist of the deep tempera of the Greek or Mediterranean isles; clouds and mountains deal in soft pastels, curtains of rain parting to show earth and heaven reflecting one another, exchanging or blending their shades. Sunsets are superb; rainbows frequent and vivid as they are in Scotland.

Stretches of the country today in the west and the north are as treeless, harsh and barren as the mountains of Judæa and the burned-out hills of Palestine, but in Patrick's time they were thickly wooded. The timber line ascended higher on the slopes of the mountains that ring the coasts of the island. Within this ring lies a shallow bowl of plain, meadow and rich, rolling pasture land studded with lakes and laced with silver streams. The Ireland of today offers some of the most beguiling country in the world. How much more lovely and pristine must it have been fifteen hundred years ago when the two-horsed, two-wheeled chariot of St Patrick criss-crossed it.

Head north from Dublin and there is hardly anywhere you go where you might not be treading in the footsteps of St Patrick and looking upon the same purple mountains and rich green pasture lands and ridges that he saw. Slane, Tara, Trim and Donaghpatrick, all connected with the Saint and his comings and going, form a rectangle no more than fifteen miles north of the capital city, and legend has Patrick visiting the site of Dublin itself when that city was no more than the Ford of the Hurdles, crossing the River Liffey, the river now spanned by famed O'Connell Bridge.

From Wicklow, northwards to Belfast and Larne Loughs, the rough, pebbled beaches of Ireland's east coast knew the grating of the keel of Patrick's ship—St Patrick's Isle, off Skerries, Gormanston, Carlingford, Strangford. The vagaries of the sea have altered the coastline and these ports of call beyond recognition, but that most beautiful of all Irish land-falls, the melancholy mass of the Mountains of Mourne, is as it was when first Patrick set eyes upon them.

Patrick's first work was in the north-east in what is now Counties Down and Antrim, wherein are located Saul of Dichu's barn, Downpatrick, Raholp and the district in and about Slemish. Here were most likely already a scattering of Christians and Christian settlements. The area about Wicklow in the south was supposed to be the seat of the first Christians in Ireland, the Scots to whom Palladius was sent, but Strangford Lough was a far better harbour; it was the seat of a thriving trade with both Britain and France and abounded in merchants, sailors and sea captains who had been in contact with that great power of the West, Rome, and its Christian religion. Here, too, and farther north by Larne, the slaves would have been landed from the slave raids, and, since these raids punished the Gallic and British coasts, the captives would have been nominally Christians.

With a foothold in Dalaradia, Patrick moved down into Meath for his challenge of the High King, and, once permission had been wrung from Laoghaire to preach throughout his domain, there was sufficient to keep the Saint busy, for Tara in Meath was the heartbeat of pre-Christian Ireland.

It was no city, but a gigantic fortress and palace topping a low, flat-topped hill, or rather ridge, the feature of which is the site, discernible as a long, shallow depression in the ground, of the High King's banquet and assembly hall which was some seven hundred feet long. In its heyday it could seat a thousand guests. A wide passage ran down the centre with two rows of tables in each section. Fourteen huge doors gave access. Fifty stewards and fifty footmen seated the guests according to their rank, their shields being hung up behind their seats. Three hundred waiters served the dishes of some three hundred cooks. The guests clad in crimson and purple cloaks, fine linen and dressed leather, gold armbands, necklaces, pins and brooches and jewels were as brilliant a sight as any court ever afforded.

This was Tara. All the buildings and stockades were of wood, protected by deep circular ditches.

From Tara, or its vicinity as a base, Patrick founded churches at Dunshauglin, Donaghpatrick and Ath Bron, as well as many others, and went upon expeditions farther afield.

One of these was to answer another challenge and one actually more dangerous to his life or limb than his bearding of the High King, who from all accounts was a well-educated and politically astute monarch. But what took Patrick north-west into the neighbourhood of what is now Ballinamore in Leitrim in the midst of the plain of Magh Sleacht, was the presence there of the chief idol of the Irish, the Stone Crom-Cruach, covered over with gold and silver and surrounded by twelve other idols covered with brass.

Legend and, not impossibly, fact, has Patrick overthrowing this idol. If he did so, it was quite the bravest act of his ministry, for he had struck at the heart of Irish superstition and made himself enemies by the tens of thousands. The character of Patrick leaves no doubt but that, if such a violent and unpolitic gesture was necessary, he had the courage to do it.

Patrick is all about Roscommon, that pastoral county of fine black soil and sweet grass, flowering rhododendrons and yellow gorse, marshy sumps and bogs, low hills, dips and hollows. Fine cattle-fattening country. Here he appeared at Boyle, at Frenchpark, at Elphin, Oran and Selce, and he was a visitor to the Royal Rath of the King of Connacht, Rath-croghan, second in power to the High King, and legendary site of the equally legendary Queen Maeve.

St Patrick's visits to the Kingdom of Connacht, which embraced Roscommon, Sligo and Mayo, were many and brought him once more into sight of the Atlantic, but this time to those places and that ocean beyond which no man lived. It is a long arm of the sea that thrusts eighteen miles inwards from Sligo Bay to the foot of the Knockarea, that astonishing stone mountain in the shape of an inverted bowl with the curious little mound atop it which is reputed to be Maeve's grave.

The rolling ocean he saw from northern Tirawley by Killala, probably standing upon the very promontory now named Downpatrick Head. In the vicinity is another hamlet of Crosspatrick, indicating that the Saint once preached and established his church there. And this was wilderness, both of sea and of land, mountains and bogs and rushing torrents, cliffs descending sheer to the boiling sea, and the inhabitants, even as now, sparse, shy and primitive compared to the east-coast culture.

It was this farthest west, by Westport, Croagh Patrick and Clew Bay—he is supposed even to have taken ship to visit the farthest removed fisherfolk of Caher Island—that Patrick referred to when he said he had carried the gospel into places and baptised heathen and ordained clergy where none had ever penetrated before on such an errand. If Christian missionaries had visited Ireland before Patrick and Christian settlements been established, it is certain that none of them had penetrated the western wilderness trodden by Patrick and his companions.

He established a church at Aghagower, passed by Lough Mask to Cong where once a great Abbey stood, and took ship on Lough Corrib, that vast lake which has an outlet to Galway Bay, today still teeming with salmon and monster brown cannibal trout. They are there in sufficient quantity and heft to please even Patrick, who was pictured by unflattering and wool-witted biographers as an impatient and vindictive fisherman who promptly overlaid the waters where the fish refused to bite with a resounding Christian malediction. From Cong it would have been no distance at all to the savage grandeur of the iron coast of Connemara.

He went northwards into Donegal, that most endearing

and dramatic of all of Eire's counties, a land of glens, mountains, tarns, woods and peat bogs, people of more than usual sweetness and charm, and a coastline gouged by the hand of some giant with the salt sea biting thirty miles inland via Lough Swilly. The famed Isle of Arran is hard by the rim of Donegal.

Patrick's voice was heard, his cross raised, in mid-Ireland in Leinster whose men were the arch-enemies of King Laoghaire of Meath. He passed through Tipperary to reach Cashel where he baptised the King's son on the stone of Patrick, which stone, or a reasonable facsimile thereof, you may see to this day. This was the chieftain whose foot was pierced by Patrick's over-enthusiastic crozier.

In the far north he looked upon the Giant's Causeway where he established many churches amongst the Picts of Dalriada; southwards he penetrated as far as Fermoy in South Cork, abutting Waterford, and there is reason to believe that he looked across the mouth of the River Shannon, the great artery of Eire that he had forded so often in his wanderings up and down and across the nation.

And if you wished to pinpoint that very centre of Ireland visited by the Saint, you would select the great plain of limestone and moorland known then as the Kingdom, and now as the County of Offaly, where the Slieve Bloom Mountains rise to relieve the endless brown vista of the moors.

It is in Offaly that the legend of the self-sacrificing Odran is set. King Foilge Berraide had never forgiven Patrick for the overthrow of the idol Crom Cruach and had sworn to kill him. Patrick's household had learned of the plot but concealed it from him. But as they entered the territory, Odran said to Patrick: 'Since I am a long time charioteering for thee, O master Patrick, let me today sit in the chief seat and do thou be charioteer.' Patrick did so. Thereafter Foilge went and gave a spear thrust through Odran in the shape of Patrick.

When Patrick began to blast Foilge with a curse, the dying Odran diverted it to a tree, showing Christian forgiveness. Nevertheless, God took up the matter at once, according to *The Tripartite Life*, struck Foilge dead and he was transported to hell.

Was this one of the twelve plots or dangers referred to by Patrick? One will never know. But an interesting and evident kernel of truth is that Patrick was an able chariot-driver and could replace his professional.

II

THE journeys were numerous and were made over a considerable period of time. Many of them were repeats when the Saint returned to churches already founded to see how they were faring and to check the work of the native priest or bishop whom he had left there.

A whole volume might be devoted to pursuing his routes and naming the communities where he preached or founded churches, leaving in his wake innumerable crosses, hills, wells, mounds, rocks, 'chairs,' footprints, etc.; the Irish place-names adapted to modern language have a wonderful lilt to them, but they are too many, and to list them might be tedious.

Bishop Tirechàn in his eighth-century compilation of the travels of the Saint and the churches founded by him names many of them and there are more details of his voyages in the eleventh-century *Tripartite Life*, though of course there is some doubt as to the accuracy of the latter, myth and legend having had five centuries to accumulate. Even Tirechàn's account is not entirely free from the suspicion of 'colouring' to suit what he thought his superiors might like to read into his account.

Available, too, are books by antiquarians and scholars of recent times who have identified the *Loca Patriciana* in terms of modern Irish geography and maps, so that a wanderer wishing to take up the trail of the Saint and look upon scenes and conformations of the land, lakes and rivers approximately as they appeared to the eyes of Patrick may do so to the enchantment of his own eyes and the uplift of his soul.

Yet, even without such scholarly aids, it is hardly possible to sit upon rocky mountain or gentle hill in Ireland, or tread the springy turf, without treading ground once walked upon by those tireless feet. For no soldier of the church, as these extraordinary men of peace are sometimes called, ever before or since left such a personal imprint upon a land as did Saint Patrick. They are not marked or sign-posted by government, or historical societies (to the eternal astonishment of the traveller in search of Patrick), but they are indelibly marked in the living memory of man.

Pause at any cross-roads hamlet, village or parish in modern Ireland in the areas known to have been evangelised by the Saint, seek out the priest or local schoolmaster or oldest inhabitant where it was that Patrick paused, and you will be shown a low mound or a bubbling spring, a rock, a cleft, a pillar, the ruins of a church, an ancient fortress site surrounded by a ditch, a depression in a meadow, a cross, an odd-shaped stone, an old graveyard, a circle of dolmens or a corbelled well. And you will hear the story that goes with it of what Patrick did, or what happened to him there.

And for truth of what is seen and said, you may take that he *did* pass by there once, that he paused to do his work, to preach, exhort, bless, baptise, teach, or with cassock and tunic removed bent his back to the erection of yet another church to the eternal love and glory of God.

Upon one of these trips, he halted in the Kingdom of Daire to found the Church of Armagh, the great Episcopal See and supposed personal See of Patrick, about which controversies have raged, and still are unsettled, to this day. Armagh is the seat of the Primate of the Church of Ireland. The controversy is pointed up by the fact that Armagh today is a city of two cathedrals. One, the Church of Ireland or Protestant Cathedral, stands upon a hill, the supposed site of the original foundations of Patrick's church. It is called St Patrick's Cathedral. On an adjoining hill rears the Roman Catholic Church, seat of the Cardinal. It, too, is known as St Patrick's Cathedral.

There seems to be no real evidence that St Patrick ever intended this charming and gentle little town built by the quiet River Callan close to the ancient Navan Fort, stronghold of Queen Macha, ever to be so distinguished. If Patrick ever mentioned it, the document is amongst those lost. Even Muirchu, writing for his superior, a Bishop of Armagh, tells only the hand-me-down tale of the circumstances of Patrick's founding his church there. There are preserved a set of Canons of church laws, supposedly promulgated by Patrick and a synod of Armachian bishops and signed by them, but the chronologies and known *floruit*s or life spans of the signatories conflict and scholars are not satisfied with the documents.

Muirchu, narrating the establishment of Patrick's church —or, as we shall see, churches—at Armagh, becomes enmeshed in Druid-Irish legend and magic and moral-pointing anecdote. Patrick asked King Daire for a piece of high ground known as the Ridge of the Willows as a place 'for the exercise of his religion.' Daire, who as we have seen from the Grazacham story had a sense of values where his property was concerned, gave Patrick instead a piece of lower land, which in Muirchu's time had become the Graves (or The Church) of the relics, near Ardd-Machae.

Upon that site today there stands oddly enough the doric-porticoed Georgian building of the Bank of Ireland, certainly an exception to the rule that ecclesiastical buildings are always raised upon the ruins or foundations of earlier religious edifices or ceremonial grounds.

This is really one of the more astonishing phenomena having to do with the curious disregard of the Irish for sites and places which one would imagine to be preserved as equally holy and sacred to those attributed to other Saints of perhaps lesser stature. For a bank is hardly the shrine to rear over the bones of Ireland's own Apostle, and that of his unfortunate sister Lupait, or Lupita, as well. The Ardmachians firmly believe that St Patrick is buried in their city, and this information is included in the Official Handbook, issued by the Urban District Council of Armagh, which, under the heading 'St Patrick's Burial Place,' states: 'In Scotch Street, where a handsome Georgian building houses the Bank of Ireland, is the site of Patrick's first Church in Armagh and the place where his sister, St Lupita, was buried. It is also the resting-place of the Saint himself; so very many ancient manuscripts speak of the burial of the Saint here as to completely refute the legend [of later date] that he is buried in Downpatrick in County Down.'

No mention is made in the little prospectus, however, that this is that same Lupita over whom, according to *The Tripartite Life*, as well as local legend already quoted, Patrick drove the wheels of his chariot three times before she died, because 'Patrick was enraged with his sister, namely Lupait, for the sin of lust which she committed so that she became pregnant.' However, in this case the hagiographers of both the eleventh and the twentieth centuries are probably equally inaccurate.

Muirchu's tale is further embellished with an anecdote which at least throws light on the importance of property rights in those days. Daire, as we have noted already, had something of the Indian giver in his make-up, for, having ceded the bit of low-lying ground to the Christians, he sent a groom to pasture a fine horse there. 'And Patrick was offended at the horse trespassing this way on his ground; and he said that Daire had done a foolish thing in sending brute beasts to disturb the holy place which he gave to God.'

The groom refused to take notice and left the horse there overnight. The next morning when he came, it was dead. He reported this to Daire who, even more choleric than Patrick, said: 'Let him be slain, too; go ye now and kill him.'

As the executioners were on their way, Daire was felled by a stroke. And here it was that the ever-present and practical queen took over again. The picture was at once clear. She sent servants to halt the killers and beg Patrick to forgive and relent. Patrick sent holy water. Horse and Daire were sprinkled. Both recovered and were as good as new. And shortly thereafter occurred the incident of the imported bronze three-gallon pot and Patrick's reiterated 'Grazacham' which convinced Daire once and for all that he had here a truly steadfast and unchangeable man who would have his way sooner or later, but in the end, have it he would.

There is a strange sweetness to the epilogue to this story: 'And that is the city which is now called Ardd-Machae. And they went both of them out, St Patrick and Daire, to inspect the admirable and acceptable gift that was being offered [the piece of high ground on the Ridge of the Willows]; and they ascended that high ground and found a hind with her little fawn lying where now stands the altar of the Northern Church in Ardd-Machae.

'And St Patrick's companions wanted to take the fawn and kill it; but the Saint did not wish this to be done, and would not allow it; nay, on the contrary, the Saint himself took the fawn and carried it on his shoulders. And the hind followed him, like a gentle and tame sheep, until he let the fawn loose in another wood situated on the north side of Ardd-Machae, where to this very day, the learned say, there are certain signs of his power.'

The locals also say that it is where St Patrick loosed the fawn he had rescued (from those most doubtful companions) that the present Catholic cathedral stands.

Within two centuries, Ardd-Machae, or Armagh, was the chief ecclesiastical city and a seat of learning as well as authority. The nubbin of the controversy which still carries on is: was it Saint Patrick's intention to have this so, or was this the work of a group of later saints and bishops who in a sense 'took over' Patrick's work and foundation and moulded it to their own design, as the later Franciscans captured the order from Francis, that gentle and humble little saint who only tried to live, think and behave like Christ.

It was the contention of the late Professor Bury that Armagh could never have gained its pre-eminent position in so short a time had it not had the original impetus of being chosen by Patrick as his seat of authority in Ireland. As for Patrick's choice of this location, instead of one more centrally located in Meath where so much of his work was done and from which there was greater access to his outlying churches, Professor Bury believed that in all probability Daire, King of Oriel, was one of the few important Irish monarchs to embrace Christianity and that it was a matter of prestige as well as protection for Patrick to establish his episcopal see close to this wealthy and powerful king.

Another view is that of Professor Kenney in his *Sources for the Early History of Ireland*, namely that the Ulidian Churches of northern Ireland were not monastic and suffered from the rise of Church Leagues. In self-defence, they 'invented' Patrick, that is to say Patrick's founding of Armagh as his own See and seat of authority, and the churches became united in Patrick.

Whatever the truth, it lies buried beneath the weight of fifteen centuries and the dust of long-dead prelates who can no longer speak and whose written words have mostly been swept away by the tides of invasion or consumed in the holocausts of fires set by men in religious contention.

Yet, for all of the powerful tradition linking Patrick with Armagh and the sincere beliefs of its inhabitants in the remains of the Saint somewhere in their midst, Patrick somehow has managed to elude this proud episcopal city, except for his presence at that touching little well on the old coach road at the outskirts of the city where the rags of the pilgrim visitors flutter from the branches of the faerie thorn that grows from the side of the hill above the Green Road of St Patrick.

The two vying cathedrals on opposite hilltops do not suggest the spirit of this man-of-one-purpose, his modesty and his self-effacement. In Downpatrick, on a less imposing hill, is another grave where his remains are supposed to have been laid, and it is on the gentle ridges of Saul, by his first-love church of Dichu's barn within view of the sea, that in all probability he breathed his last. At any rate, the early Armachian propagandists had to invent a legend that showed why he did *not* die at Armagh, even though he wished to do so.

It was not an Armachian bishop, according to Muirchu, who administered the last rites to Patrick when his hour at *Sabul* (Saul) had come, but his old artisan, Tassach, make of patens, credence tables and altar-chalices, for the hundreds of churches reared by Patrick. Now raised to the eminence of bishop, he gave the weary old Apostle the final communion and held for him the Cross that for the last time his eyes might rest upon it. It was Tassach then who closed those eyes when the great soul had fled.

But the men of Armagh had a final word in the death legend. In return for obeying the angel, four petitions were to be granted to Patrick, and the first of these was, according to Muirchu: 'That thy jurisdiction be in Ardd-Machae.' *The Tripartite Life* is even more explicit and detailed: 'It hath been granted to thee by God,' saith the Angel, 'that thy dignity and thy pre-eminence, thy piety and thy teaching, shall be in Armagh as if thou thyself were alive therein.'

Patrick then replies in a kind of love poem dedicated to Armagh:

> 'I have chosen a place of resurrection,
> Armagh my church:
> I have no power over my freedom,
> It is in bondage to the end
> It is Armagh that I love,
> A dear thorpe, a dear hill
> A fortress which my soul haunteth;
> Emain of the heroes will be waste.'

Now, oddly, Emain, that Irish hill built up of layer upon layer of the history of heroes, *is* waste, in the sense that there is no building of any kind upon it. It is a high, green mound surrounded by a fosse still twenty feet in depth in parts, and from which stands of huge oaks have sprouted.

G

But the legend of its desertion goes back to a far older curse. Emain Macha for seven hundred years was the seat of the warrior kings of Ulster and their Knights of the Red Branch who in legendary deed and renown were to Ireland what the Knights of the Round Table were to Britain.

But eventually the Irish High King at Tara warred upon the Ulster kingdom and sent his young kin, the three Collas, to give battle. They defeated the Ulstermen and drove them eastwards to the lands that are now Down and Antrim. The great Navan Fort of Emain Macha was destroyed, militarily, though the hill and fosse remained. But so great had been the slaughter and so thorough the destruction that bad cess hung about the place, and later generations that gave rise to Daire shunned the place and built their Duns on the twin hills a mile away where they could look down upon the remains of the unfortunate Emain, and still do.

The angel who forbade Patrick to die at Armagh also arranged for the place of Patrick's burial in this manner:

'Now, when the angel came to him, he gave him advice as to the manner of his burial: let two unbroken oxen be chosen, and let them go whithersoever they will, and in whatever place they lie down, let a church be built in honour of thy poor body.

'And as the angel said, restive bullocks were chosen, and they drew a wagon, with a litter firmly fixed on it in which the holy body was, yoked to their shoulders. And oxen from the herds of Conail, from that place that is called Clocher, on the east of Findubair, were made glorious by being chosen for this purpose. And they went forth, the will of God guiding them to Dun-da-leth-glaisse, where Patrick was buried.'

Thus, the last earthly voyage of Patrick the Saint.

CHAPTER NINE

The Living Patrick

I

SPIDDAL in Connemara is a wide place in the road that runs due west from Galway along Galway Bay, that body of the Atlantic whose mouth suffers permanent blockade by the chain of the Isles of Aran.

The beach is not a proper one as we think of beaches, but tumbled rocks that climb up out of the sea as though some giant had been shovelling gravel. This is one of those points in Ireland, farthest west, beyond which, as Patrick wrote, there lives no one.

The inhabitants are desperately poor, for there is nothing much hereabouts to make a living from but the summer visitors. They speak Gaelic more than English. Back in the hills, a few who have mastered the old trick of avoiding the revenuers brew potheen in private stills, but the energy even for this trade seems to be dying out.

The people have the exhausted air of being the sole survivors of the shipwreck of Ireland. They, with the exception of the inhabitants of northern Donegal, the northernmost tip of the Island, are also, by direct and unspoiled descent, the oldest of the Irish and the nearest to their noble and hardy ancestors who peopled the wilderness of this region when first Patrick toiled into the darkness of that farthest west holding aloft the torch of his faith.

One night in recent times a party was given on the beach

at midnight where a peat fire was built within a ring of stones a few feet above the black, sparkling sea. The potables consisted of some bottles of Irish whiskey, but the central attraction was a vast keg of stout, black as the night sea itself and creamy with froth as the edge of the sea was rimmed with foam. For provender there were *crobeans*—pigs' trotters —cooking in water borrowed from the ocean, and another great black pot of potatoes bubbling away in the same sea water. In place of the traditional harpist there was an ardent jongleur in collarless shirt and jacket with an accordion and a prodigious memory for the music of his land.

The entire village, young and old, from bent gaffers to nursing babes, came to the party, though not exactly invited, but they were welcomed for this was Ireland and the notion of having the party without them in the first place was absurd.

There were the stars shining into the sea, a hundred yards or so from the road that ran through the village, and atop the dark, tumbled rocks the orange glow of the peat fire. Strains of music topped the lapping of the wavelets and drifted over to the community, and besides, earlier on, a giant of a man, Shaun, the road worker, had been seen proceeding thither bearing a keg upon his shoulders, and he had not returned. By twos and threes and fives of families, the villagers naturally drifted over to see what was toward and remained. Soon all were there and the *Feis* or feast got under way.

Shaun, the road worker, the strong man, was built and thewed like that Macc Cairthinn the champion and strong man of St Patrick who bore his master aloft on his shoulders across the fords of the Shannon and the Liffey. He was called into service for there was no man of the original cast of the party capable of so much as lifting the keg more than six inches off the ground, much less whipping it on to his shoulders and proceeding with it in the dusk for more than a hundred yards of track over rocks, sand and broken shells.

Night had not yet quite completed its descent when Shaun appeared from the road bearing the barrel. In those northern latitudes in the summer, the green glow lingers around the edges of the horizon. Against this was silhouetted in pure black cut-out the gigantic figure of this man, taller even by the width of the keg borne so lightly on his shoulders. He was a giant, a hero out of Ireland's past, and because of his coming, his slow, stately walk beneath his burden, the present slipped away the more quickly and did not return again that night.

He set the cask down as gently as though it were made of egg-shells. His eyes gleamed in the firelight, the eyes of such a gentle giant, and he passed the back of his hand across his parched lips. The keg was broached immediately and the first glass of smooth, dark velvet vanished soundlessly and at one long tug down his throat. His exhalation of contentment momentarily out-sighed the sea.

All then gathered about the fire-ring. The lemony-orange glow that is peculiar to burning peat illuminated their faces. Only the dress was modern. The faces, the attitudes, the rhymes they spoke and the songs they sang in mournful Gaelic were as ancient as the basalt blocks on which they sat. The songs were of love and heroes, of gallantry and treachery, of ambush and fighting against odds, about living and dying. In them were the sounds of clashing arms, cries of joy and of agony, and the awful death-rattle of hanged men. It was a gathering of the Celts, a night for musicians, bards, singers and poets.

Warm and cheery as is the glow of peat and an outdoor

fire made of this combustible turf, there is something ineffably sad about its burning, for in a sense it is the burning of the skin of Ireland, the burning up of Ireland itself, as though now the staunch ship which had borne them all for so long and through such fearful tempests, wrecked at last, must be itself consumed by those whom she has carried so bravely through so much. Tears seem to lie close to the surface in this part of the world. It is a country for which it is not difficult to weep.

As the spirit moved them, those about the fire struck up songs, sometimes accompanied by the musician, sometimes in chorus *a-capella*, often a single voice unaccompanied raised in some old lament full of drama and pain, and shivers of old wrongs remembered ran through the crowd, even though the peat embers were fiercely hot.

To mend the mood, the accordionist swung into something light-footed and merry. A group of village children, young girls, little female savages with the faces of angels beneath the smudges from fire, crobeans and potato skins, detached themselves and, forming at the top of a great, flat stone, danced through the figures of foursome and eightsome reels. There is something indescribably moving when this dance is performed by the very young, their little bodies stiff and straight as ramrods, arms hanging limp and motionless by their sides, faces blank and expressionless, the eyes seeming to gaze inwards, and only the busy feet twinkling in and out of the figures carrying the stiffly poised forms through oddly touching patterns. All but the feet seem to be a part of a strange, dreamy detachment. That night on the Connemara shore the centuries melted away and the *Sidhe*, the faerie folk, were dancing within a magic circle. A moon had risen, and the rigid little forms cast rigid little moon shadows.

It needed then, one knew, but the coming of Patrick,

white-cowled, tonsured, with cross and crozier, as the Druids
had prophesied:

> 'Adzehead will come over a furious sea;
> His mantle head-holed, his staff crook-headed
> His altar in the east of his house
> All his household shall answer
> *Amen, amen!*'

—to send the little dancing figures back to the mythology
that created them, vanishing into the shimmering night and
leaving bare the flat rock to be trod by the tireless, sandal-
shod feet of God's personal messenger to the Irish. Music
and song would be stilled. He would speak, and soon those
wonderful, carved-in-wood faces of the old, like mahogany
in the firelight, and the fresh countenances and eager eyes
of the young would be dissolved in tears, as they were in
the old days, fifteen hundred years ago, under the spell of
the sincerity of his eloquence and the story he told them of
the One who gave His life on the Cross that others might be
saved.

The village of Cong, from the Irish *Cunga*, meaning a
narrow neck of land, lies indeed as such between two great
bodies of fresh water, Lough Mask to the north and the
greater Lough Corrib to the south. A river connects the
two; and, eventually, Corrib, by means of another river,
empties into Galway Bay.

Cong is in the County of Mayo and was once an important
centre of learning in the Kingdom of Connacht. In the year
1106 a great Abbey was built there—the ruins of which may
still be visited—and a school of learning which at one time
harboured no less than three thousand scholars. The famous
Cross of Cong, an exquisite piece of native art and workman-

ship, now in the Dublin Museum, was connected with this Abbey, though the 'Yellow Crozier,' as it is called, made of oak covered with bronze and silver plates engraved and adorned with enamel and filigree gold, came originally from nearby Tuam where the archbishop of Connacht had his seat.

But the tides of time and the religious wars have swept over Cong and what was once a great ecclesiastical centre of piety and learning is now a dusty, impoverished village of two streets and a small widening of the road that might be designated a village square, before the entrance to the ruins of the Abbey and Ashford Castle.

The series of disasters that overtook Ireland from the coming of the Norsemen, the English invasion and the great famine of modern times have left their marks upon Cong. Some of the houses in the main village street would appear to have been bombed, for only the empty walls stand with their roofs fallen in. But no bombs fell here; the roofs decayed, there was no money to repair them; the people who had lived there simply moved away. The empty shells of houses remained. The place seems to have given up. Beyond a few bits of fishing tackle for sale, the inhabitants do not make even the attempt to cash in on the tourists and guests who come to visit or stay at the huge Ashford Castle Hotel, that extraordinary pile, a fourteenth-century castle built for a rich man in the nineteenth century.

Yet, at the time of the Procession of Corpus Christi, the little village comes to life. For days before, the children have been out in the woods gathering green boughs and making garlands of field flowers, and these now are used to decorate the houses, along with strips of coloured bunting and holy pictures of Christ and the Virgin Mary put up over the doorways or in the windows.

But it is during the procession itself, which begins behind the ruins of the Abbey, winding across the bridge to the village square, pausing for a celebration of the Mass before an altar set up there and making then the circuit before returning to the Abbey, that an astonishing phenomenon takes place. There is *literally not a soul left in the village*. All the inhabitants, joined by the owners and staff of the nearby great hotel, *are* in the procession.

As the Mass is celebrated on the little rise of ground by the old well in the glare of the hot sun, the men in their rusty black suits, the women in their shawls, and the children garbed in the white cotton of innocence, kneel in the dust. A community in its entirety is kneeling there in a unity of faith and spirit; no one is left out except on the fringe an occasional guest or spectator of another faith lacking the grace and courtesy of older civilisations which made it a point to honour and be polite to the gods of others where they were worshipped.

Under the blue Irish sky the priests chant, the little bells tinkle, the sun splinters from the Host and the regalia, bared heads are bowed . . . and Patrick is there.

One cannot look upon the scene, the white vestments of the celebrating priests shining against the background of green-garlanded grey houses, the kneeling men, women and children, without thinking upon the Saint whose work this was.

For the worship, the giving up of self, the total devotion and dedication, be it only of the moment, of one and all alike, the rich and the poor, the great and the small, is yet today in Ireland a reflection of the power of dedication and sincerity of faith that Patrick brought with him when he came to evangelise the heathen, and which from the time of his own discovery of the meaning of God on the lonely slopes of Sliabh Miss was the ruling passion of his life and the key to his existence. There is a quality in Irish Catholicism and the Irish Church that traces directly back through fifteen centuries to Saint Patrick, the purity and catholicity of his beliefs and the steadfastness of purpose with which he disseminated them amongst a people more than ready to receive them.

Rarely has a man expended so much vital force, or commanded so much spiritual power, or left behind him so much of his character and spiritual drive almost as a reserve or store-house to which later generations might repair to draw upon the still living strength of a man already long dead.

Patrick would have approved the hundred-per-cent participation and dedication of the little village of Cong to the festival in honour of the Eucharist, for he was never less than that in his own devotion and sacrifice.

The history of Ireland from the seventh century or so on downwards to modern times has been one long, melancholy tragedy culminating in a paradise of a land that has been almost emptied of its once great people and the land-loving and ambitious youth that is needed to restore and nourish a country's greatness. Some have accused the Church of contributing to this tragedy, but an overall view of the indignities and injustices inflicted upon the Irish people, physically, politically and spiritually, down through the ages does not bear this out. But for the breath of Patrick to sustain them, they could not have survived to the extent that they have today, to emerge once more as an independent nation. One cannot even say that there were times when nothing but their religion was left to them, for even that was taken away from them, or rather the practice of it and it was forced to go underground. But the faith never wavered.

Patrick had proved too strong for even the cruel and insensate march of history and the rapacious men who make it.

And this finally was the imperishable legacy that Patrick left to the 'Scots who believed in Christ'—himself. He was a foreigner, a stranger who came into their midst, but once he was there, he gave himself wholly, and he provided the volatile heroic people of that country with an example that a man could follow. What sustained the Irish, what must sustain any man in no matter what desperate straits, was the triumph of Patrick against all odds and the belief he gave them by example in God.

The service of God has never been easy. God not only accepts the persons of those devoted men who offer themselves, but tries them bitterly during that service and often unto their deaths. Yet He stands by them, too, through hardships and perils that would destroy an ordinary person. Patrick was not an ordinary person. God set his seal upon him and Patrick made his own indelible mark upon the people to whom he was sent.

The story of Patrick is one of a great and ultimate triumph, a triumph achieved by a man who was not cast in any hero's mould, who was human and sometimes humanly weak. He was often sorely tried by the vicissitudes of life, but he never once wavered in his faith and trust in God and therefore never faltered upon the appointed way.

However distorted the picture of Patrick developed by legend and the myth-makers during succeeding centuries, each generation through its own bitter trials could not help but find comfort and itself sustained, not only by the promises of the faith that Patrick had brought them, but by the examples from his own life of the size of the mountains that can be moved by prayer and that faith.

That real Patrick of the *Confessio* and the *Letter*, who not only led the Irish to God, but showed them so convincingly how that God was to be loved, worshipped and served, truly stirred the hearts of the men and women of Ireland in that far-off century of his mission to them; and it has continued to do so to this day.

In his physical lifetime St Patrick never deserted the Irish. He has not deserted them ever since, in his continuing spiritual immortality. The angel who turned him from the road to Armagh when his death was nigh promised him that, if he obeyed, he should sit in judgement upon all the Irish on the Day of Resurrection. The Irish are well content to have it so. They will find no more forgiving, loving or honourable judge.

CONFESSION

&

LETTER
TO THE SOLDIERS
OF COROTICUS

CONFESSION*

I AM Patrick, a sinner, most unlearned, the least of all the faithful, and utterly despised by many. My father was Calpornius, a deacon, son of Potitus, a priest, of the village Bannavem Taburniae; he had a country seat nearby, and there I was taken captive.

I was then about sixteen years of age. I did not know the true God. I was taken into captivity to Ireland with many thousands of people—and deservedly so, because we turned away from God, and did not keep His commandments, and did not obey our priests, who used to remind us of our salvation. And the Lord *brought over us the wrath of His anger and scattered us among many nations*, even *unto the utmost part of the earth*, where now my littleness is placed among strangers.

2. And there *the Lord opened the sense of my unbelief* that I might at last remember my sins and *be converted with all my heart to the Lord my God*, who *had regard for my abjection*, and mercy on my youth and ignorance, and watched over me before I knew Him, and before I was able to distinguish between good and evil, and guarded me, and comforted me as would a father his son.

3. Hence I cannot be silent—*nor, indeed, is it expedient*—about the great benefits and the great grace which the Lord has deigned to bestow upon me *in the land of my captivity;* for this we can give to God in return after having been chastened by Him, *to exalt and praise His wonders* before *every nation that is* anywhere *under the heaven*.

* *Confession* and *Letter to the Soldiers of Coroticus* are from the translation by Ludwig Bieler, published by Longmans, Green & Co. reproduced with their kind permission.

4. Because there is no other God, nor ever was, nor will be, than God the Father unbegotten, without beginning, from whom is all beginning, the Lord of the universe, as we have been taught; and His son Jesus Christ, whom we declare to have always been with the Father, spiritually and ineffably begotten by the Father before the beginning of the world, before all beginning; and by Him are made all things visible and invisible. He was made man, and, having defeated death, was received into heaven by the Father; *and He hath given Him all power over all names in heaven, on earth, and under the earth, and every tongue shall confess to Him that Jesus Christ is Lord and God*, in whom we believe, and whose advent we expect soon to be, *judge of the living and of the dead*, who will render to every man according to his deeds; and *He has poured forth upon us abundantly the Holy Spirit, the gift* and *pledge* of immortality, who makes those who believe and obey *sons of God* and *joint heirs with Christ;* and Him do we confess and adore, one God in the Trinity of the Holy Name.

5. For He Himself has said through the Prophet: *Call upon me in the day of thy trouble, and I will deliver thee, and thou shalt glorify me.* And again He says: *It is honourable to reveal and confess the works of God.*

6. Although I am imperfect in many things, I nevertheless wish that my brethren and kinsmen should know what sort of person I am, so that they may understand my heart's desire.

7. I know well *the testimony of my Lord*, who in the Psalm declares: *Thou wilt destroy them that speak a lie.* And again He says: *The mouth that belieth killeth the soul.* And the same Lord says in the Gospel: *Every idle word that men shall speak, they shall render an account for it on the day of judgment.*

8. And so I should dread exceedingly, *with fear and*

trembling, this sentence on that day when no one will be able to escape or hide, but we all, without exception, shall have *to give an account* even of our smallest sins *before the judgment seat of* the Lord *Christ*.

9. For this reason I long had in mind to write, but hesitated until now; I was afraid of exposing myself to the talk of men, because I have not studied like the others, who thoroughly imbibed law and Sacred Scripture, and never had to change from the language of their childhood days, but were able to make it still more perfect. In our case, what I had to say had to be translated into a tongue foreign to me, as can be easily proved from the savour of my writing, which betrays how little instruction and training I have had in the art of words; for, so says Scripture, *by the tongue will be discovered the wise man, and understanding, and knowledge, and the teaching of truth*.

10. But of what help is an excuse, however true, especially if combined with presumption, since now, in my old age, I strive for something that I did not acquire in youth? It was my sins that prevented me from fixing in my mind what before I had barely read through. But who believes me, though I should repeat what I started out with?

As a youth, nay, almost as a boy not able to speak, I was taken captive, before I knew what to pursue and what to avoid. Hence today I blush and fear exceedingly to reveal my lack of education; for I am unable to tell my story to those versed in the art of concise writing—in such a way, I mean, as my spirit and mind long to do, and so that the sense of my words expresses what I feel.

11. But if indeed it had been given to me as it was given to others, then I would not be silent *because of my desire of thanksgiving*, and if perhaps some people think me arrogant for doing so in spite of my lack of knowledge and my slow

H

tongue, it is, after all, written: *The stammering tongues shall quickly learn to speak peace.*

How much more should we earnestly strive to do this, we, who are, so Scripture says, *a letter of Christ for salvation unto the utmost part of the earth*, and, though not an eloquent one, yet . . . *written in your hearts, not with ink, but with the spirit of the living God!* And again the Spirit witnesses that *even rusticity was created by the Highest*.

12. Whence I, once rustic, exiled, unlearned, who does not know how to provide for the future, this at least I know most certainly that before I was humiliated I was like a stone lying in the deep mire; and He that is mighty came and in His mercy lifted me up, and raised me aloft, and placed me on the top of the wall. And therefore I ought to cry out aloud and so also render something to the Lord for His great benefits here and in eternity—benefits which the mind of men is unable to appraise.

13. Wherefore, then, be astonished, *ye great and little that fear God*, and you men of letters on your estates, listen and pore over this. Who was it that roused up me, the fool that I am, from the midst of those who in the eyes of men are wise, and expert in law, and powerful in word and in everything? And He inspired me—me, the outcast of this world—before others, to be the man (if only I could!) who, *with fear and reverence and without blame*, should faithfully serve the people to whom the love of Christ conveyed and gave me for the duration of my life, if I should be worthy; yes indeed, to serve them humbly and sincerely.

14. In the light, therefore, of our faith in the Trinity I must make this choice, regardless of danger I must make known the gift of God and everlasting consolation, without fear and frankly I must spread everywhere the name of God so that after my decease I may leave a bequest to my brethren

and sons whom I have baptised in the Lord—so many thousands of people.

15. And I was not worthy, nor was I such that the Lord should grant this to His servant; that after my misfortunes and so great difficulties, after my captivity, after the lapse of so many years, He should give me so great a grace in behalf of that nation—a thing which once, in my youth, I never expected nor thought of.

16. But after I came to Ireland—every day I had to tend sheep, and many times a day I prayed—the love of God and His fear came to me more and more, and my faith was strengthened. And my spirit was moved so that in a single day I would say as many as a hundred prayers, and almost as many in the night, and this even when I was staying in the woods and on the mountain; and I used to get up for prayer before daylight, through snow, through frost, through rain, and I felt no harm, and there was no sloth in me—as I now see, because the spirit within me was then fervent.

17. And there one night I heard in my sleep a voice saying to me: 'It is well that you fast, soon you will go to your own country.' And again, after a short while, I heard a voice saying to me: 'See, your ship is ready.' And it was not near, but at a distance of perhaps two hundred miles, and I had never been there, nor did I know a living soul there; and then I took to flight, and I left the man with whom I had stayed for six years. And I went in the strength of God who directed my way to my good, and I feared nothing until I came to that ship.

18. And the day that I arrived the ship was set afloat, and I said that I was able to pay for my passage with them. But the captain was not pleased, and with indignation he answered harshly: 'It is of no use for you to ask us to go along with us.' And when I heard this, I left them in order to return to

the hut where I was staying. And as I went, I began to pray; and before I had ended my prayer, I heard one of them shouting behind me, 'Come, hurry, we shall take you on in good faith; make friends with us in whatever way you like.' And so on that day I refused to suck their breasts for fear of God, but rather hoped they would come to the faith of Jesus Christ, because they were pagans. And thus I had my way with them, and we set sail at once.

19. And after three days we reached land, and for twenty-eight days we travelled through deserted country. And they lacked food, and hunger overcame them; and the next day the captain said to me: 'Tell me, Christian: you say that your God is great and all-powerful; why, then, do you not pray for us? As you can see, we are suffering from hunger; it is unlikely indeed that we shall ever see a human being again.'

I said to them full of confidence: '*Be* truly *converted with all your heart to the Lord my God*, because nothing is impossible for Him, that this day He may send you food on your way until you be satisfied; for He has abundance everywhere.' And, with the help of God, so it came to pass: suddenly a herd of pigs appeared on the road before our eyes, and they killed many of them; and there they stopped for two nights and fully recovered their strength, and their hounds received their fill, for many of them had grown weak and were half-dead along the way. And from that day they had plenty of food. They also found wild honey, and offered some of it to me, and one of them said: 'This we offer in sacrifice.' Thanks be to God, I tasted none of it.

20. That same night, when I was asleep, Satan assailed me violently, a thing I shall remember *as long as I shall be in this body*. And he fell upon me like a huge rock, and I could not stir a limb. But whence came it into my mind,

ignorant as I am, to call upon Helias? And meanwhile I saw the sun rise in the sky, and while I was shouting 'Helias! Helias!' with all my might, suddenly the splendour of that sun fell on me and immediately freed me of all misery. And I believe that I was sustained by Christ my Lord, and that His Spirit was even then crying out in my behalf, and I hope it will be so *on the day of my tribulation*, as is written in the Gospel: *On that day*, the Lord declares, *it is not you that speak, but the Spirit of your Father that speaketh in you.*

21. And once again, after many years, I fell into captivity. On that first night I stayed with them. I heard a divine message saying to me: 'Two months will you be with them.' And so it came to pass: on the sixtieth night thereafter *the Lord delivered me out of their hands.*

22. Also on our way God gave us food and fire and dry weather every day, until, on the tenth day, we met people. As I said above, we travelled twenty-eight days through deserted country, and the night that we met people we had no food left.

23. And again after a few years I was in Britain with my people, who received me as their son, and sincerely besought me that now at last, having suffered so many hardships, I should not leave them and go elsewhere.

And there I saw in the night the vision of a man, whose name was Victoricus, coming as it were from Ireland, with countless letters. And he gave me one of them, and I read the opening words of the letter, which were, 'The voice of the Irish'; and as I read the beginning of the letter I thought that at the same moment I heard their voice—they were those beside the Wood of Voclut, which is near the Western Sea —and thus did they cry out *as with one mouth:* 'We ask thee, boy, come and walk among us once more.'

And I was quite broken in heart, and could read no further,

and so I woke up. Thanks be to God, after many years the Lord gave to them according to their cry.

24. And another night—whether within me, or beside me, *I know not, God knoweth*—they called me most unmistakably with words which I heard but could not understand, except that at the end of the prayer He spoke thus: '*He that has laid down His life for thee*, it is He that speaketh in thee'; and so I awoke full of joy.

25. And again I saw Him praying in me, and I was as it were within my body, and I heard Him above me, that is, over *the inward man*, and there He prayed mightily with groanings. And all the time I was astonished, and wondered, and thought with myself who it could be that prayed in me. But at the end of the prayer He spoke, saying that He was the Spirit; and so I woke up, and remembered the Apostle saying: *The Spirit helpeth the infirmities of our prayer. For we know not what we should pray for as we ought; but the Spirit Himself asketh for us with unspeakable groanings, which cannot be expressed in words;* and again: *The Lord our advocate asketh for us.*

26. And when I was attacked by a number of my seniors who came forth and brought up my sins against my laborious episcopate, on that day indeed was I struck so that I might have fallen now and for eternity; but the Lord graciously spared the stranger and sojourner for His name and came mightily to my help in this affliction. Verily, not slight was the shame and blame that fell upon me! I ask God that *it may not be reckoned to them as sin.*

27. As cause for proceeding against me they found— after thirty years!—a confession I had made before I was a deacon. In the anxiety of my troubled mind I confided to my dearest friend what I had done in my boyhood one day, nay, in one hour, because I was not yet strong. *I know*

not, God knoweth—whether I was then fifteen years old; and I did not believe in the living God, nor did I so from my childhood, but lived in death and unbelief until I was severely chastised and really humiliated, by hunger and nakedness, and that daily.

28. On the other hand, I did not go to Ireland of my own accord, not until I had nearly perished; but this was rather for my good, for thus was I purged by the Lord; and He made me fit so that I might be now what was once far from me—that I should care and labour for the salvation of others, whereas then I did not even care about myself.

29. On that day, then, when I was rejected by those referred to and mentioned above, in that night I saw a vision of the night. There was a writing without honour against my face, and at the same time I heard God's voice saying to me: 'We have seen with displeasure the face of Deisignatus' (thus revealing his name). He did not say, 'Thou hast seen,' but, 'We have seen,' as if He included Himself, as He sayeth: *He who toucheth you toucheth as it were the apple of my eye*.

30. Therefore *I give Him thanks who hath strengthened me* in everything, as He did not frustrate the journey upon which I had decided, and the work which I had learned from Christ my Lord; but I rather felt after this no little strength, and my trust was proved right before God and men.

31. And so I say boldly, my conscience does not blame me now or in the future: God is my witness that I have not lied in the account which I have given you.

32. But the more am I sorry for my dearest friend that we had to hear what he said. To him I had confided my very soul! And I was told by some of the brethren before that defence—at which I was not present, nor was I in Britain, nor was it suggested by me—that he would stand up for me in my absence. He had even said to me in person:

'Look, you should be raised to the rank of bishop!'—of which I was not worthy. But whence did it come to him afterwards that he let me down before all, good and evil, and publicly, in a matter in which he had favoured me before spontaneously and gladly—and not he alone, but the Lord, who *is greater than all?*

33. Enough of this. I must not, however, hide God's gift which He bestowed upon me *in the land of my captivity;* because then I earnestly sought Him, and there I found Him, and He saved me from all evil *because*—so I believe—*of His Spirit that dwelleth* in me. Again, boldly said. But God knows it, had this been said to me by a man, I had perhaps remained silent for the love of Christ.

34. Hence, then, I give unwearied thanks to God, who kept me faithful *in the day of my temptation,* so that today I can confidently offer Him my soul as a living sacrifice—to Christ my Lord, who *saved me out of all my troubles.* Thus I can say: '*Who am I, O Lord,* and to what hast Thou called me, Thou who didst assist me with such divine power that today *I* constantly *exalt* and magnify Thy name *among the heathens* wherever I may be, and not only in good days but also in tribulations? So indeed I must accept with equanimity whatever befalls me, be it good or evil, and always give thanks to God, who taught me to trust in Him always without hesitation, and who must have heard my prayer so that I, however ignorant I was, *in the last days* dared to undertake such a holy and wonderful work—thus imitating somehow those who, as the Lord once foretold, would preach His Gospel *for a testimony to all nations* before *the end of the world.* So we have seen it, and so it has been fulfilled: indeed, we are witnesses that the Gospel has been preached unto those parts beyond which there lives nobody.

25. Now, it would be tedious to give a detailed account

of all my labours or even a part of them. Let me tell you briefly how the merciful God often freed me from slavery and from twelve dangers in which my life was at stake— not to mention numerous plots, which I cannot express in words; for I do not want to bore my readers. But God is my witness, who knows all things even before they come to pass, as He used to forewarn even me, poor wretch that I am, of many things by a divine message.

36. *How came I by this wisdom*, which was not in me, who neither *knew the number of my days* nor knew what God was? Whence was given to me afterwards the gift so great, so salutary—to know God and to love Him, although at the price of leaving my country and my parents?

37. And many gifts were offered to me in sorrow and tears, and I offended the donors, much against the wishes of some of my seniors; but, guided by God, in no way did I agree with them or acquiesce. It was not grace of my own, but God, who is strong in me and resists them all—as He had done when I came to the people of Ireland to preach the Gospel, and to suffer insult from the unbelievers, *hearing the reproach of my going abroad*, and many persecutions even unto bonds, and to give my free birth for the benefit of others; and, should I be worthy, I am prepared to give even my life without hesitation and most gladly for His name, and it is there that I wish to spend it until I die, if the Lord would grant it to me.

38. For I am very much God's debtor, who gave me such great grace that many people were reborn in God through me and afterwards confirmed, and that clerics were ordained for them everywhere, for a people just coming to the faith, whom the Lord took from the utmost parts of the earth, as He once had promised through His prophets: *To Thee the gentiles shall come from the ends of the earth and shall say: 'How*

false are the idols that our fathers got for themselves, and there is no profit in them'; and again: *I have set Thee as a light among the gentiles, that Thou mayest be for salvation unto the utmost part of the earth.*

39. And there I wish to wait for His promise who surely never deceives, as He promises in the Gospel: *They shall come from the east and the west, and shall sit down with Abraham and Isaac and Jacob*—as we believe the faithful will come from all the world.

40. For that reason, therefore, we ought to fish well and diligently, as the Lord exhorts in advance and teaches, saying: *Come ye after me, and I will make you to be fishers of men.* And again He says through the prophets: *Behold, I send many fishers and hunters, saith God,* and so on. Hence it was most necessary to spread our nets so that a great multitude and throng might be caught for God, and that there be clerics everywhere to baptise and exhort a people in need and want, as the Lord in the Gospel states, exhorts, and teaches, saying: *Going therefore now, teach ye all nations, baptising them in the name of the Father, and the Son, and the Holy Spirit, teaching them to observe all things whatsoever I have commanded you: and behold I am with you all days even to the consummation of the world.* And again He says: *Go ye therefore into the whole world, and preach the Gospel to every creature. He that believeth and is baptised shall be saved; but he that believeth not shall be condemned.* And again: *This Gospel of the kingdom shall be preached in the whole world for a testimony to all nations, and then shall come the end.* And so too the Lord announces through the prophet, and says: *And it shall come to pass, in the last days, saith the Lord, I will pour out of my Spirit upon all flesh; and your sons and your daughters shall prophesy, and your young men shall see visions, and your old men shall dream dreams. And upon my servants indeed, and upon my handmaids will I pour out in*

those days of my Spirit, and they shall prophesy. And in Osee He saith: 'I will call that which was not my people, my people; . . . and her that had not obtained mercy, one that hath obtained mercy. And it shall be in the place where it was said: "You are not my people," there they shall be called the sons of the living God.'

41. Hence, how did it come to pass in Ireland that those who never had a knowledge of God, but until now always worshipped idols and things impure, have now been made a people of the Lord, and are called sons of God, that the sons and daughters of the kings of the Irish are seen to be monks and virgins of Christ?

42. Among others, a blessed Irishwoman of noble birth, beautiful, full-grown, whom I had baptised, came to us after some days for a particular reason: she told us that she had received a message from a messenger of God, and he admonished her to be a virgin of Christ and draw near to God. Thanks be to God, on the sixth day after this she most laudably and eagerly chose what all virgins of Christ do. Not that their fathers agree with them; no—they often even suffer persecution and undeserved reproaches from their parents; and yet their number is ever increasing. How many have been reborn there so as to be of our kind, I do not know—not to mention widows and those who practice continence.

But greatest is the suffering of those women who live in slavery. All the time they have to endure terror and threats. But the Lord gave His grace to many of His maidens; for, though they are forbidden to do so, they follow Him bravely.

43. Wherefore, then, even if I wished to leave them and go to Britain—and how I would have loved to go to my country and my parents, and also to Gaul in order to visit the brethren and to see the face of the saints of my Lord! God knows it that I much desired it; but I am bound by the

Spirit, who gives evidence against me if I do this, telling me that I shall be guilty; and I am afraid of losing the labour which I have begun—nay, not I, but Christ the Lord who bade me come here and stay with them for the rest of my life, if the Lord will, and will guard me from every evil way that I may not sin before Him.

44. This, I presume, I ought to do, but I do not trust myself *as long as I am in this body of death,* for strong is he who daily strives to turn me away from the faith and the purity of true religion to which I have devoted myself to the end of my life to Christ my Lord. But the hostile flesh is ever dragging us unto death, that is, towards the forbidden satisfaction of one's desires; and I know that in part I did not lead a perfect life as did the other faithful; but I acknowledge it to my Lord, and do not blush before Him, because I lie not: from the time I came to know Him in my youth, the love of God and the fear of Him have grown in me, and up to now, thanks to the grace of God, I have kept the faith.

45. And let those who will, laugh and scorn—I shall not be silent; nor shall I hide the signs and wonders which the Lord has shown me many years before they came to pass, as He knows everything even *before the times of the world.*

46. Hence I ought unceasingly to give thanks to God who often pardoned my folly and my carelessness, and on more than one occasion spared His great wrath on me, who was chosen to be His helper and who was slow to do as was shown me and as the Spirit suggested. And the Lord had mercy on me thousands and thousands of times because He saw that I was ready, but that I did not know what to do in the circumstances. For many tried to prevent this my mission; they would even talk to each other behind my back and say: 'Why does this fellow throw himself into danger among enemies who have no knowledge of God?' It was

not malice, but it did not appeal to them because—and to this I own myself—of my rusticity. And I did not realise at once the grace that was then in me; now I understand that I should have done so before.

47. Now I have given a simple account to my brethren and fellow servants who have believed me because of what I said and still say in order to strengthen and confirm your faith. Would that you, too, would strive for greater things and do better! This will be my glory, for *a wise son is the glory of his father.*

48. You know, and so does God, how I have lived among you from my youth in the true faith and in sincerity of heart. Likewise, as regards the heathen among whom I live, I have been faithful to them, and so I shall be. God knows it, I have overreached none of them, nor would I think of doing so, for the sake of God and His Church, for fear of raising persecution against them and all of us, and for fear that through me the name of the Lord be blasphemed; for it is written: *Woe to the man through whom the name of the Lord is blasphemed.*

49. *For although I be rude in all things,* nevertheless I have tried somehow to keep myself safe, and that, too, for my Christian brethren, and the virgins of Christ, and the pious women who of their own accord made me gifts and laid on the altar some of their ornaments; and I gave them back to them, and they were offended that I did so. But I did it for the hope of lasting success—in order to preserve myself cautiously in everything so that they might not seize upon me or the ministry of my service, under the pretext of dishonesty, and that I would not even in the smallest matter give the infidels an opportunity to defame or defile.

50. When I baptised so many thousands of people, did I perhaps expect from any of them as much as half a screpall?

Tell me, and I will restore it to you. Or when the Lord ordained clerics everywhere through my unworthy person and I conferred the ministry upon them free, if I asked any of them as much as the price of my shoes, *speak against me and I will return it to you.*

51. On the contrary, I spent money for you that they might receive me; and I went to you and everywhere for your sake in many dangers, even to the farthest districts, beyond which there lived nobody and where nobody had ever come to baptise, or to ordain clergy, or to confirm the people. With the grace of the Lord, I did everything lovingly and gladly for your salvation.

52. All the while I used to give presents to the kings, besides the fees I paid to their sons who travel with me. Even so they laid hands on me and my companions, and on that day they eagerly wished to kill me; but my time had not yet come. And everything they found with us they took away, and me they put in irons; and on the fourteenth day the Lord delivered me from their power, and our belongings were returned to us because of God and our dear friends whom we had seen before.

53. You know how much I paid to those who administered justice in all those districts to which I came frequently. I think I distributed among them not less than the price of fifteen men, so that you might enjoy me, and I might always enjoy you in God. I am not sorry for it—indeed it is not enough for me; I still spend and shall spend more. God has power to grant me afterwards *that I myself may be spent for your souls.*

54. Indeed, *I call God to witness upon my soul that I lie not;* neither, I hope, am I writing to you in order to make this an occasion of flattery or covetousness, nor because I look for honour from any of you. Sufficient is the honour that is

not yet seen but is anticipated in the heart. *Faithful is He that promised; He never lieth.*

55. But I see myself exalted even in the present world beyond measure by the Lord, and I was not worthy nor such that He should grant me this. I know perfectly well, though not by my own judgment, that poverty and misfortune becomes me better than riches and pleasures. For Christ the Lord, too, was poor for our sakes; and I, unhappy wretch that I am, have no wealth even if I wished for it. Daily I expect murder, fraud, or captivity, or whatever it may be; *but I fear none of these things* because of the promises of heaven. I have cast myself into the hands of God Almighty, who rules everywhere, as the prophet says: *Cast thy thought upon God, and He shall sustain thee.*

56. So, now *I commend my soul to my faithful* God, *for whom I am an ambassador* in all my wretchedness; but God *accepteth no person,* and chose me for this office—to be, although among His least, one of His ministers.

57. Hence let me *render unto Him for all He has done to me.* But what can I say or what can I promise to my Lord, as I can do nothing that He has not given me? May He *search the hearts and reins;* for greatly and exceedingly do I wish, and ready I was, that He should give me His chalice to drink, as He gave it also to the others who loved Him.

58. Wherefore may God never permit it to happen to me that I should lose His people which He purchased in the utmost parts of the world. I pray to God to give me perseverance and to deign that I be a faithful witness to Him to the end of my life for my God.

59. And if ever I have done any good for my God whom I love, I beg Him to grant me that I may shed my blood with those exiles and captives for His name, even though I should be denied a grave, or my body be woefully torn to pieces

limb by limb by hounds or wild beasts, or the fowls of the air devour it. I am firmly convinced that if this should happen to me, I would have gained my soul together with my body, because on that day without doubt we shall rise in the brightness of the sun, that is, in the glory of Christ Jesus our Redeemer, as sons of the living God and *joint heirs with Christ, to be made conformable to His image;* for *of Him, and by Him, and in Him* we shall reign.

60. For this sun which we see rises daily for us because He commands so, but it will never reign, nor will its splendour last; what is more, those wretches who adore it will be miserably punished. Not so we, who believe in, and worship, the true sun—Christ—who will never perish, nor will he *who doeth His will;* but he *will abide for ever as Christ abideth for ever,* who reigns with God the Father Almighty and the Holy Spirit before time, and now, and in all eternity. Amen.

61. Behold, again and again would I set forth the words of my confession. *I testify* in truth and in joy of heart *before God and His holy angels* that I never had any reason except the Gospel and its promises why I should ever return to the people from whom once before I barely escaped.

62. I pray those who believe and fear God, whosoever deigns to look at or receive this writing which Patrick, a sinner, unlearned, has composed in Ireland, that no one should ever say that it was my ignorance if I did or showed forth anything however small according to God's good pleasure; but let this be your conclusion and let it so be thought, that—as is the perfect truth—it was the gift of God. This is my confession before I die.

LETTER TO THE SOLDIERS OF COROTICUS

I, PATRICK, a sinner, unlearned, resident in Ireland, declare myself to be a bishop. Most assuredly I believe that what I am I have received from God. And so I live among barbarians, a stranger and exile for the love of God. He is witness that this is so. Not that I wished my mouth to utter anything so hard and harsh; but I am forced by the zeal for God; and the truth of Christ has wrung it from me, out of love for my neighbours and sons for whom I gave up my country and parents and *my life to the point of death*. If I be worthy, I live for my God to teach the heathen, even though some may despise me.

2. With my own hand I have written and composed these words, to be given, delivered, and sent to the soldiers of Coroticus; I do not say, to my fellow citizens, or to fellow citizens of the holy Romans, but to fellow citizens of the demons, because of their evil works. Like our enemies, they live in death, allies of the Scots and the apostate Picts. Dripping with blood, they welter in the blood of innocent Christians, whom I have begotten into the number for God and confirmed in Christ!

3. The day after the newly baptised, anointed with chrism, in white garments (had been slain)—the fragrance was still on their foreheads when they were butchered and slaughtered with the sword by the above-mentioned people—I sent a letter with a holy presbyter whom I had taught from his childhood, clerics accompanying him, asking them to let us

have some of the booty, and of the baptised they had made captives. They only jeered at them.

4. Hence I do not know what to lament more: those who have been slain, or those whom they have taken captive, or those whom the devil has mightily ensnared. Together with him they will be slaves in Hell in an eternal punishment; for *who committeth sin is a slave* and will be called *a son of the devil*.

5. Wherefore let every God-fearing man know that they are enemies of me and of Christ my God, *for whom I am an ambassador*. Parricide! fratricide! *ravening wolves that eat the people of the Lord as they eat bread!* As I said, *The wicked, O Lord, have destroyed Thy law*, which but recently He had excellently and kindly planted in Ireland, and which had established itself by the grace of God.

6. I make no false claim. I share in the work of those *whom He called and predestinated* to preach the Gospel amidst grave persecutions *unto the end of the earth*, even if the enemy shows his jealousy through the tyranny of Coroticus, a man who has no respect for God nor for His priests whom He chose, giving them the highest, divine, and sublime power, that *whom they should bind upon earth should be bound also in heaven*.

7. Wherefore, then, I plead with you earnestly, *ye holy and humble of heart*, it is not permissible to court the favour of such people, nor to take food or drink with them, nor even to accept their alms, until they make reparation to God in hardships, through penance, with shedding of tears, and set free the baptised servants of God and handmaids of Christ, for whom He died and was crucified.

8. *The most High disapproveth the gifts of the wicked. . . . He that offereth sacrifice of the goods of the poor, is as one that sacrificeth the son in the presence of his father. The riches*, it is

written, *which he has gathered unjustly, shall be vomited up from his belly; the angel of death drags him away, by the fury of dragons he shall be tormented, the viper's tongue shall kill him, unquenchable fire devoureth him.* And so—*Woe to those who fill themselves with what is not their own;* or, *What doth it profit a man that he gain the whole world, and suffer the loss of his own soul?*

9. It would be too tedious to discuss and set forth everything in detail, to gather from the whole Law testimonies against such greed. Avarice is a deadly sin. *Thou shalt not covet thy neighbour's goods. Thou shalt not kill.* A murderer cannot be with Christ. *Whosoever hateth his brother* is accounted *a murderer.* Or, *He that loveth not his brother abideth in death.* How much more guilty is he that has stained his hands with the blood of the sons of God whom He has of late purchased in the *utmost part of the earth* through the call of our littleness!

10. Did I come to Ireland without God, or according to the flesh? Who compelled me? I am bound by the Spirit not to see any of my kinsfolk. Is it of my own doing that I have holy mercy on the people who once took me captive and made away with the servants and maids of my father's house? I was freeborn according to the flesh. I am the son of a decurion. But I sold my noble rank—I am neither ashamed nor sorry—for the good of others. Thus I am a servant in Christ to a foreign nation for the unspeakable glory *of life everlasting which is in Christ Jesus our Lord.*

11. And if my own people do not know me, *a prophet hath no honour in his own country.* Perhaps we are not *of the same fold* and have not *one and the same God as father,* as is written: *He that is not with me, is against me, and he that gathereth not with me, scattereth.* It is not right that *one destroyeth,* another buildeth up. *I seek not the things that are mine.*

It is not my grace, but God *who has given this solicitude into my heart*, to be one of His hunters or fishers whom God once foretold would come in the last days.

12. I am hated. What shall I do, Lord? I am most despised. Look, Thy sheep around me are torn to pieces and driven away, and that by those robbers, by the orders of the hostile-minded Coroticus. Far from the love of God is a man who hands over Christians to the Picts and Scots. *Ravening wolves* have devoured the flock of the Lord, which in Ireland was indeed growing splendidly with the greatest care; and the sons and daughters of kings were monks and virgins of Christ—I cannot count their number. Wherefore, *be not pleased with the wrong done to the just; even to hell it shall not please.*

13. Who of the saints would not shudder to be merry with such persons or to enjoy a meal with them? They have filled their houses with the spoils of dead Christians, they live on plunder. They do not know, the wretches, that what they offer their friends and sons as food is deadly poison, just as Eve did not understand that it was death she gave to her husband. So are all that do evil: they work death as their eternal punishment.

14. This is the custom of the Roman Christians of Gaul: they send holy and able men to the Franks and other heathen with so many thousand *solidi* to ransom baptised captives. You prefer to kill and sell them to a foreign nation that has no knowledge of God. You betray the members of Christ as it were into a brothel. What hope have you in God, or anyone who thinks as you do, or converses with you in words of flattery? God will judge. For Scripture says: *Not only they that do evil are worthy to be condemned, but they also that consent to them.*

15. I do not know what I should say or speak further about the departed ones of the sons of God, whom the

sword has touched all too harshly. For Scripture says: *Weep with them that weep;* and again: *If one member be grieved, let all members grieve with it.* Hence the Church mourns and laments her sons and daughters whom the sword has not yet slain, but who were removed and carried off to faraway lands, where sin abounds openly, grossly, impudently. There people who were freeborn have been sold, Christians made slaves, and that, too, in the service of the abominable, wicked, and apostate Picts!

16. Therefore I shall raise my voice in sadness and grief: O you fair and beloved brethren and sons whom I have begotten in Christ, countless of number, what can I do for you? I am not worthy to come to the help of God or men. *The wickedness of the wicked hath prevailed over us. We have been made,* as it were, *strangers.* Perhaps they do not believe that we have received one and the same baptism, or have one and the same God as father. For them it is a disgrace that we are Irish. *Have ye not,* as is written, *one God? Have ye, every one of you, forsaken his neighbour?*

17. Therefore I grieve for you, I grieve, my dearly beloved. But again, I rejoice within myself. I have not laboured for nothing, and my journeying abroad has not been in vain. And if this horrible, unspeakable crime did happen—thanks be to God, you have left the world and have gone to Paradise as baptised faithful. I see you: you have begun to journey where *night shall be no more, nor mourning, nor death; but you shall leap like calves loosened from their bonds, and you shall tread down the wicked, and they shall be ashes under your feet.*

18. You, then, will reign with the apostles, and prophets, and martyrs. You will take possession of eternal kingdoms, as He Himself testifies, saying: *They shall come from the east and from the west, and shall sit down with Abraham, and Isaac, and Jacob in the kingdom of heaven. Without are dogs, and*

sorcerers, . . . and murderers; and liars and perjurers have *their portion in the pool of everlasting fire.* Not without reason does the Apostle say: *Where the just man shall scarcely be saved, where shall the sinner and ungodly transgressor of the law find himself?*

19. Where, then, will Coroticus with his criminals, rebels against Christ, where will they see themselves, they who distribute baptised women as prizes—for a miserable temporal kingdom, which will pass away in a moment? *As a cloud or smoke that is dispersed by the wind,* so *shall the* deceitful *wicked perish at the presence of the Lord; but the just shall feast with great constancy* with Christ, *they shall judge nations,* and rule over wicked kings for ever and ever. Amen.

20. *I testify before God and His angels* that it will be so as He indicated to my ignorance. It is not my words that I have set forth in Latin, but those of God and the apostles and prophets, who have never lied. *He that believeth shall be saved; but he that believeth not shall be condemned, God hath spoken.*

21. I ask earnestly that whoever is a willing servant of God be a carrier of this letter, so that on no account it be suppressed or hidden by anyone, but rather be read before all the people, and in the presence of Coroticus himself. May God inspire them sometime to recover their senses for God, repenting, however late, their heinous deeds—murderers of the brethren of the Lord!—and to set free the baptised women whom they took captive, in order that they may deserve to live to God, and be made whole, here and in eternity! Be peace to the Father, and to the Son, and to the Holy Spirit. Amen.

BIBLIOGRAPHY

ARDILL, REV. JOHN ROCHE, *St Patrick, A.D.* 180 (Hodges, Figgis & Co., Dublin, 1931).

BEDE, *A History of the English Church and People.* Translated by Leo Sherly-Price (Penguin, London, 1955).

BIELER, LUDWIG, *The Life and Legends of St Patrick, Problems of Modern Scholarship.* Review by Prof. Thomas F. O'Rahilly. (Irish Historical Studies, Vol. VIII, No. 31, March, 1953.)

BIELER, LUDWIG, *The Life and Legends of St Patrick* (Clonmore & Reynolds Ltd., Dublin, 1949).

BIELER, LUDWIG, *The Works of St Patrick.* Ancient Christian Writers, Vol. XVII. (Longmans, Green & Co., London, 1953.)

BIELER, LUDWIG, *Patrick and the Kings.* The Irish Ecclesiastical Record, March, 1956. (Browne & Nolan Co. Ltd., Dublin.)

BURY, J. B., *The Life of St Patrick and His Place in History* (MacMillan & Co. Ltd., London, 1905).

CARNEY, JAMES, *Studies in Irish Literature and History* (Dublin Institute for Advanced Studies, Dublin, 1955).

CHAMBERLAIN, G. A., *St Patrick, His Life and Work* (Church of Ireland Printing and Publishing Co., Dublin, 1932).

CHAUVIRÉ, ROGER, *History of Ireland* (Clonmore & Reynolds Ltd., Dublin, 1952).

CURTAYNE, ALICE, *Lough Derg, St Patrick's Purgatory* (Burns, Oates & Washbourn Ltd., Dublin, 1945).

CUSACK, MILDRED F., *The Life of St Patrick* (Longmans, Green & Co., London, 1871).

DILLON, MYLES, Ed. *Early Irish Society* (At The Sign of The Three Candles, Dublin, 1954).

DURANT, WILL, *The Age of Faith* (Simon & Schuster, 1950).

ESPOSITO, MARIO, *St Patrick's 'Confessio' and the 'Book of Armagh'* (Irish Historical Studies, Vol. IX, No. 33, March, 1954).

ESPOSITO, MARIO, *The Patrician Problem and a Possible Solution* (Irish Historical Studies, Vol. X, No. 38, Sept., 1956).

FERGUSON, SIR SAMUEL, *The Remains of St Patrick, Apostle of Ireland* (Sealy, Bryers & Walker, Dublin, 1888).

GAFFNEY, JOHN J., *Life of St Patrick* (Browne & Nolan Ltd., Dublin, 1932).

GOGARTY, OLIVER ST JOHN, *I Follow St Patrick* (Constable, London, 1950).

GWYNN, JOHN. Edited with Introduction and Appendices. *The Book of Armagh* (Hodges, Figgis Co. Ltd., Dublin, 1913).

HAYWARD, RICHARD, *The Corrib Country* (Dundalgan Press, Dundalk, 1954).

JOHNSTON, REV. THOMAS J., ROBINSON, VEN. JOHN L., JACKSON, VERY REV. ROBERT WYSE, *History of the Church of Ireland* (A.P.C.L., Dublin, 1953).

JOYCE, P. W., *A Social History of Ancient Ireland*, Vols. I and II (Longmans, Green & Co., London, 1903).

KENNEY, *Sources for Early Irish History*, Vol. I (Columbia University Press).

LEATHAM, DIANA, *They Built on a Rock* (Celtic Art Society, Glasgow, 1948).

LETTS, WINIFRED M., *St Patrick the Travelling Man* (Ivor Nicholson & Watson Ltd., London, 1932).

LYNCH, PATRICIA, *Tales of Irish Enchantment* (Clonmore & Reynolds Ltd., Dublin, 1952).

MACALISTER, R. A. S., *The Archæology of Ireland* (R. V. Coleman, N.Y., 1927).

MACNEILL, PROF. EOIN, *Early Irish Laws and Institutions* (Burns, Oates & Washbourn, Dublin, 1935).

MACNEILL, EOIN, *Silva Focluti*. Proceedings of the Royal Irish Academy (Hodges, Figgis Co., Dublin, 1923).

MACNEILL, EOIN, *St Patrick, Apostle of Ireland* (Dublin, 1934).

MORRIS, WILLIAM BULLEN, *Ireland and St Patrick* (M. H. Gill & Son, Dublin, 1891).

MORRIS, WILLIAM BULLEN, *The Life of St Patrick* (M. H. Gill & Son, Dublin, 1878).

MULCHRONE, KATHLEEN, *The Mission of Patricius Secundus Episcopus Scottorum*. The Irish Ecclesiastical Record, March, 1956. (Browne & Nolan Ltd., Dublin.)

O'BRIEN, E. O., *Birthplace of St Patrick* (Browne & Nolan Ltd., Dublin, 1903).

O'GRADY, STANDISH, *Finn and His Companions* (T. Fisher Unwin, London).

O'MEARA, JOHN J., *The 'Confession' of St Patrick and the 'Confessions' of St Augustine*. The Irish Ecclesiastical Record, March, 1956. (Browne & Nolan Ltd., Dublin.)

O'RAHILLY, THOMAS F., *The Two Patricks, A Lecture on the History of Christianity in Fifth-century Ireland*. Review by John F. O'Doherty. (Irish Historical Studies, Vol. III, No. 11, March, 1943.)

O'RAHILLY, THOMAS F., *The Two Patricks* (Dublin Institute for Advanced Studies, Dublin, 1942).

O'RIORDAIN, SEAN P., *Antiquities of the Irish Countryside* (Methuen & Co. Ltd., London, 1942).

PUSEY, EDWARD B., D.D. Trans. *The Confessions of St Augustine* (Pocket Books Inc., N.Y., 1952).

SHERMAN, REV. J. F., *St Patrick or Loca Patriciana* (M. H. Gill & Son, Dublin, 1882).

STOKES, WHITLEY. Ed. *The Tripartite Life of St Patrick*, Vols. I and II (H.M. Stationery Office, London, 1887).

SWIFT, EDMUND L., *The Life and Acts of St Patrick* (Hibernia Press Co., Dublin, 1809).

TODD, JAMES HENTHORN, *St Patrick, Apostle of Ireland* (Hodges, Smith & Co., Dublin, 1864).

WALLER, REV. BOLTON C., *Patrick the Man* (Association for Promotion of Christian Knowledge, Dublin, 1932).

WHITE, NEWPORT J. D., *St Patrick, His Writings and Life* (Society for Promoting Christian Knowledge, London, 1920).

WHITE, NEWPORT J. D. Trans. *The Writings of St Patrick* (S.P.C.K., London, 1954).

WHITE, CANON N. J. D., *The Teaching of St Patrick* (Association for Promotion of Christian Knowledge, Dublin, 1932).

WILDE, *Loch Corrib* (Sign of the Three Candles, Dublin, 1955. Re-issued).

WRIGHT, REV. CHARLES H. H., *The Genuine Writings of St Patrick*. Trans. (4 Bouverie St., London).

INDEX

Abraham, 111
  Wells of, 165
Achille Islands, 172
Adamnan Eleran, Bishop, 111
Aedh, Bishop, 59
Aetius, Roman Consul, 23
Aghagower, 174, 184
Aigli, Mount, 174, 176
Ailill, King, 99
Amator, Bishop, 47, 49
Amolngaid, King, 164
Angel Victor, 110
Antrim, 158–60, 166, 178, 181, 194
Apocrypha, 58
Ard Macha, 158
Ardd-Machae, 15, 189, 190, 193
  Cathedral, 191
Armagh, 72, 74, 85, 87, 103, 109, 110,
    188, 191–3, 204
  Bishop of, 188; Book of, 12, 34, 73,
    75; Cathedral, 113, 159, 163, 188;
    County Museum of, 85; Official
    Handbook issued by Urban District
    Council, 189; Seat of Primate of
    Church of Ireland, 188
Arran, Isle of, 185, 195
Ashford Castle, 200
Ath Bron, 182
Ath Truimm, 100
Auxerre, 19, 46–7, 55
  Bishop of, 50, 57
Auxilius, Bishop, 123

Baldoyle, 30
Ballinamore, 183
Ballymena, 166–7
Bannavem Taburniae, 17–8, 27
Bede, 21, 23, 35–6, 46, 57
Belfast, 27, 181
Bellanagare, 160
Benignus or Benen, 93–4, 102–3, 115,
    125–6

Bible, The, 58
Bieler, Prof. Ludwig, 12, 58, 119
Blackwatertown, 86
Book of Armagh, 12, 34, 73, 75
Boulogne, 18
Boyle, 160, 183
Boyne, 90, 99–100
Braid, valley of the, 166
Breg, plain of, 91
Brehons, 75
Bristol, 104
Britain, 20–1, 34–9, 42–3, 47, 49, 53, 56,
    97, 104, 136, 140–1, 182, 194
Brockagh, Mount, 31
Burrishoole, 172
Bury, Professor, 191

Caetiacus, 74
Caher Island, 175, 184
Calpornius, a Decurion, 17, 19, 22–3
Canaan, Mount, 168
Canne, 36
Caplait, a Druid, 163
Carlingford, 181
Carrickyvegraly Point, 175
Cashiel, a rock, 102, 185
Catholic Church, 22, 44–5, 63, 71, 74,
    79, 80, 106, 123, 188
Celestine, Roman Pontiff, 23, 35, 47, 57
Christianity, 28, 35, 47
  British, 50, 57; and Church, 17, 35,
    38; and Druids, 65; in Ireland, 11,
    31, 45, 51, 62–3, 71, 98, 122, 169,
    182, 191; State Religion, 16, 69
Ciaran, Bishop, 111
Clare, 172, 175
Clew Bay, 172, 184
Clovis, 13
Clochar, 107
Clocher, 194
Clogher, 107
Cluain Fiacnae, 87

235